Sharing
THE SUNDAY SCRIPTURES
with Youth

❖ *To Father Bob Stamschror,* ❖
a youth minister and editor
dedicated to breaking open the word of God
for our youth.

 Genuine recycled paper with 10% post-consumer waste.
Printed with soy-based ink.

The publishing team included Robert P. Stamschror, development editor;
Rebecca Fairbank, manuscript editor; Gary J. Boisvert, typesetter; Maurine R. Twait,
art director; Stephan Nagel, cover designer; pre-press, printing, and binding by the
graphics division of Saint Mary's Press.

The illustrations on pages 13, 23, 33, 47, and 67 in this book are from *Clip Art for
Year B,* by Steve Erspamer (Chicago: Liturgy Training Publications, 1993). Copyright
© 1993 by the Archdiocese of Chicago, 1800 North Hermitage Avenue, Chicago, IL
60622-1101. Used with permission. All rights reserved.

The acknowledgments continue on page 136.

Printed in the United States of America

Printing: 9 8 7 6 5 4 3 2 1

Year: 2004 03 02 01 00 99 98 97 96

ISBN 0-88489-410-X

Lectionary-Based Resources for Youth Ministry

Sharing
THE SUNDAY
SCRIPTURES
with Youth

Cycle B

Maryann Hakowski

Saint Mary's Press
Christian Brothers Publications
Winona, Minnesota

Contents

Ordinary Time

Introduction

In the beginning was the Word, and the Word was with God, and the Word was God. (John 1:1, NRSV)

Recognizing the Hunger

Today's youth are hungry.
They are hungry for the word of God.
They are hungry for the Good News of Jesus Christ.
And many of them have not had a taste of it.

The Challenge of Catholic Youth Evangelization, by the National Federation for Catholic Youth Ministry, challenges youth ministers to feed the hungers of young people. The document identifies the following hungers:
• the hunger for meaning and purpose
• the hunger for connection
• the hunger for recognition
• the hunger for justice
• the hunger for the holy

(Pp. 5–6)

By effectively sharing the word of God with young people, we can help them find purpose and meaning for their lives. They will discover that they are connected with God and with others through a faith community in which God's word is shared, explored, and lived. They will find that God recognizes the gifts of all persons and celebrates their worth. They will see that God's word really is Good News for the oppressed, and it offers the possibility of countering the materialism and consumerism that are rampant in our world. Finally, they will find that God's purpose is to make them holy.

Overview

The Lectionary

The lectionary contains the Scripture readings for all the eucharistic celebrations (Sundays and weekdays) of the liturgical year. The liturgical year, and consequently the lectionary, begins with the first Sunday of Advent. It continues through the Christmas season, after which Ordinary Time begins. Ordinary Time is interrupted by the seasons of Lent and Easter, then it resumes and continues to the end of the liturgical year.

The Sunday readings are divided into three cycles that rotate year to year. The Gospel of Matthew is used in year A, the Gospel of Mark in year B, and the Gospel of Luke in year C. The Gospel of John has a special place in the Lenten and Easter seasons of all three cycles.

Each Sunday in the lectionary includes three readings and a psalm. The first reading is typically from the Hebrew Scriptures and is selected to relate with the Gospel reading. It often foreshadows something that will happen in the Gospel, and occasionally the Gospel even quotes it. The psalm usually complements the first reading and the Gospel. The second reading is from one of the letters of the Apostles. It is not chosen for its relationship with the other readings. Rather, it is intended to provide a semi-continuous reading of all the letters over the three-year period. The third reading is the Gospel, and it is taken from one of the four Gospels in the aforementioned fashion.

The resources in this book are based on the Scripture readings in the lectionary for the Sundays of the B cycle.

Why a Lectionary Approach?

Why choose the lectionary as the basis for a Scripture resource for teens? For many Catholics—including young people—exposure to the Bible comes primarily at Mass, when the Scriptures are read from the lectionary. For these Catholics, the activities in this book will review and reinforce the scriptural word they hear on Sunday. For those who do not attend Mass regularly, this book will put them in touch with the Sunday Scriptures and may even serve as an invitation to celebrate the Word with the community in the Sunday Eucharist.

Also, the Catholic lectionary offers an organized and thorough method for listening to God's word as it comes through the Scriptures. The selection of Sunday readings for the three cycles of the liturgical year ensures that the principal portions of God's word will be heard and considered over a suitable period of time.

At the same time, *Sharing the Sunday Scriptures with Youth: Cycle B* is not intended to be an alternative to the catechetical component of a youth ministry program, nor even as a substitute for the study of the Scriptures in a catechetical component. Rather, it is intended to be a Scripture-based supplement for ongoing catechesis and other elements of a youth ministry effort. This book can also serve as a connection between youth ministry efforts and Sunday liturgical celebrations in the parish.

The Activities

Action-Centered

The Scriptures are most often experienced by reading them or listening to them and then having them explained. The resources in this book go beyond that method. By way of hands-on activities, the participants not only hear and understand God's word but are actively engaged with it and are invited to respond in a personal way.

Relevant

The activities in *Sharing the Sunday Scriptures with Youth: Cycle B* make every attempt to be authentic both to the Scriptures and to the experiences of teens living in contemporary U.S. society. With the vast experiential differences among teens of different parts of the country in mind, as well as differences in age, race, and socioeconomic status, I chose activities that relate to needs, questions, concerns, and celebrations most common to all.

The scriptural themes on which the activities are based are chosen from the Sunday readings as a set rather than on a line or phrase from just one of the readings.

Diverse

This book employs a wide variety of activities and learning methods. The following list identifies each type of activity, along with a distinguishing icon. The icons will help you quickly locate a particular type of activity that you might want to use. Some activities are a combination of more than one type.

= affirmation   = drama   = journaling   = Scripture study

= community service = family activity   = music   = storytelling

= craft   = game that teaches = prayer   = video resource

= discussion   = icebreaker   = reflection   = witness talk

The Format   The resources for each Sunday are set up in the following sequence:

Initial Information

Each set of resources begins by identifying the Sunday of the year being considered, the lectionary reading number to help one find the readings for that Sunday in the lectionary, and the Scripture citations for that Sunday.

God's Word

The "God's Word" section contains a major theme drawn from the readings and a brief synopsis of the readings. Also included in this section are several additional themes called "Themes for Teens," which connect with the lived experience of today's teens.

Our Response

"Our Response" includes one specific, detailed activity with all the information you will need to prepare and facilitate it with a group of young people. This activity is usually based on the major theme that is drawn from the Scripture readings. Also included are several pithy activity ideas for alternative activities that are related to the suggested themes and connected with one or more of the Scripture readings.

Strategies and Contexts   The resources in this book can be used in many ways and in many settings. Select the way that appropriately addresses your setting and best engages your group of teens. Here are some possible uses:
- as starting points for weekly youth group meetings
- as Scripture-related supplements for youth group meetings
- as a general resource for planning retreats and lock-ins, or as quick ideas for meetings
- as aids for youth ministers who grapple with the Scriptures themselves, to ease their fears of using Scripture-related activities with young people
- as Scripture- and liturgy-related supplements for high school religion teachers, especially in courses on the Scriptures, the Mass, or the liturgical year
- as a homily help for pastors preparing for youth liturgies or any parish liturgy

Advantages   Using a lectionary-based resource with an activities approach has a number of advantages, including the following:

Excites Catholic youth about Scripture study. Most teens could think of at least ten things they would rather do than read the Bible. This book provides a variety of fun, exciting, and challenging ways of experiencing the Scriptures.

Engages youth with the Scriptures. The Bible is a whole library of books of different literary forms, so it can be intimidating at first glance. Most teens have no idea where to begin or even why they should open the Bible. The activities in this book give young people a taste of what is inside the Bible and an invitation to read more.

Promotes a lifelong habit of spending time with the Scriptures. Experiencing God's word in a more personal and meaningful way can encourage young people to make the Bible a lifelong companion.

Introduces the Scriptures as a tool for building relationships with God and others. The Scriptures include wonderful recipes for how to live in relationship with others and how to relate to God. Teens are always struggling with relationships. They are often pulling away from parents and moving toward peers. This resource pays special attention to relationships with one's self, others, and God.

Encourages adults who work with youth to spend more time with the Scriptures. Many adults working with youth—especially volunteers—are intimidated by anything related to the Scriptures or prayer. A synopsis of the Scripture readings for each Sunday is provided to familiarize such persons with the readings and to help them use the learning activities to open the Word with young people.

Makes spending time with the Scriptures exciting and meaningful. Approaching the Scriptures with a sense of adventure invites teens to unlock the mysteries found there. With some guidance and creative ways for unlocking these mysteries, teens will be encouraged to delve into them to find meaning for themselves.

Explores symbols and rituals found in the Scriptures. Taking part in the activities in this book, especially the prayer experiences, allows young people to experience the rich symbolism in the passages they read. They will discover, firsthand, connections between Catholic rituals and rituals portrayed in the Scriptures.

Helps young people experience the Scriptures as good news in a world filled with bad news. Young people today are in great need of hope. They see many reasons for despair as they look around at their families, their communities, and their world. The Scriptures can help them discover and celebrate the goodness in themselves and others as well as the good news of salvation through Jesus Christ.

Begins with the Bible message. Many youth Bible programs begin with critical issues facing youth and try to weave the Bible in where they can. This resource is different in that it *begins* with the Scriptures and relates its message to developmental, relational, and societal issues in the lives of teens.

Enables teens to make connections between the Scriptures and their own life. The Scriptures come alive when they find expression in life. The activities in this book engage teens and help them actively apply the Scriptures to their own experience.

Proclaims the Good News effectively and enables young people to proclaim the Good News in return. Sharing the Scriptures with young people is only the beginning of evangelization. Jesus preached the Word to his disciples, related it to their lives, and taught them how to share it. This resource helps young people find the language and the courage to share the Good News with others.

Limitations

Using a lectionary-based approach to exploring the Scriptures with youth has some limitations. First, a strict lectionary-based approach—one that always uses the resources for the current Sunday—may not match the needs and circumstances of a particular group of young people at a particular time. It may be necessary to look to another Sunday's readings—or even a Scripture passage not in the lectionary—for a theme and activities that speak to a current happening.

Second, the Scripture readings chosen for the three cycles of the Catholic lectionary do not encompass all the readings in the Bible. Studying only the Scriptures included in the lectionary ignores a number of books of the Bible, especially some of those in the Hebrew Scriptures.

Finally, the resources found here are by no means designed to replace the liturgy of the word at Mass. And though it may be true, unfortunately, that many teens do not attend liturgy on Sunday, this sharing of the Scriptures should be a means of inviting them back to Mass rather than a replacement or excuse for missing Mass.

The Challenge

In her book *Fashion Me a People*, Maria Harris suggests that the key to Scripture study is knowing the Word, interpreting the Word, living the Word, and doing the Word (pp. 60–61).

Our challenge is to enable young people to experience the Word, grapple with its meaning, connect it to their own life, share it with their peers, and find the courage to respond to the God revealed in it.

Being a minister of the Word to young people is challenging, but it is eye opening and exciting, too. One cannot help but be changed in experiencing the Scriptures through the eyes of a young person.

One of my favorite Scripture passages is the one in which Jesus feeds the hungry with both the word of God and bread and fish, blessed and shared.

We need the word of God, blessed and shared, to fill our hunger. May God bless you in your ministry and nourish you and your young people as you share the word of God together.

And the Word became flesh and lived among us. (John 1:14, NRSV)

Advent

First Sunday of Advent

Scripture Readings (2)
- ❖ Isa. 63:16–17,19; 64:2–7
- ❖ Ps. 80:2–3,15–16,18–19
- ❖ 1 Cor. 1:3–9
- ❖ Mark 13:33–37

God's Word

A major theme of the Scripture readings is "Come, Lord, come."

In the first reading, Isaiah presents to the Lord a people who have become so unfaithful that they need a powerful and merciful God who will take the initiative to save them. Isaiah wishes that God would find the people doing what is right, but in fact, they are filled with guilt for their sins. Isaiah acknowledges that God is their Father-Creator who has saved them in the past, and he asks God to come to their rescue, as God would do for people who turn to the Lord and wait for the Lord to come.

The psalmist also recognizes the need for God to take the initiative in saving the people. If God will send someone who—as one of them—will turn away from what is wrong and look on the face of God, the whole people will be saved.

For Paul, the beginning of the salvation that the psalmist hoped for has been realized in Jesus. He begins the First Letter to the Corinthians with an acknowledgment of this blessing of grace and peace that has come from God through Jesus. For the Corinthians it is now a time to wait faithfully, trusting in the fullness of salvation still to come.

The Gospel reading echoes the theme of faithful waiting. Jesus tells the parable of a man who goes away to a far-off country, leaves his servants in charge, and then returns unexpectedly. Jesus uses this parable to deliver a wake-up call to the disciples. He tells them to remain on guard because the Master might return at any time.

As we start the Advent season, we long for Jesus to come and be with us so that we may turn our life more fully and completely to God. We pray, "Come, Lord, come."

Themes for Teens

The following themes from the Scriptures relate to the lives of teens:
- You are the potter; we are the clay.
- Turn around to Christ.
- God's deeds are amazing.
- Wake up; Jesus is coming.
- We wait for the Lord.

Our Response

Activity **Wake-up Service**

This prayer service is keyed to the Gospel reading. It invites the young people to think of Advent as a time to wake up and take a close look at their life.

Before the prayer service, obtain an old-fashioned alarm clock with bells on the top. Wind it up so that it is set to ring.

Gather the young people in a circle in the prayer space, with only a small table in the center. Place the alarm clock on the table.

Begin the prayer service with verse 1 of the song "City of God," by Dan Schutte (*Glory and Praise,* vol. 3 [Phoenix, AZ: North American Liturgy Resources, 1982], no. 187).

Next, read Mark 13:33–37.

After the reading, pull the alarm stop and let the alarm ring until it is finished. Say, "The Lord is coming. Are you awake?"

Take time for quiet reflection and then close with the second verse of "City of God."

Activity Ideas

The following activity ideas also relate to the Scripture readings. You may want to read the passage(s) indicated as part of the activity.

- Buy some inexpensive clay or play dough and allow the teens some time to work with it. Read the last passage from the first reading, where it says that God is the potter and we are the clay. Have the teens pretend they are God, creating each person as someone special. Direct them to create a symbol of the person they hope to be. (Isa. 63:16–17,19; 64:2–7)

- When Paul greets the Corinthians, it is with the beautiful blessing, "Grace and peace from God our Father and the Lord Jesus Christ." How do we greet one another? When your group members arrive, ask them to go around to each person in the room and greet him or her. The only catch is that they must use a different greeting for each person. Afterward, ask them how they can make people in the group feel more welcome. How can they extend a greeting to newcomers as warm as Paul's blessing? (1 Cor. 1:3–9)

- If the young people are unfamiliar with the Advent wreath, introduce them to this tradition. Together, bless the Advent wreath and light the first candle as a sign of waiting in hope for Christ to come. Plan to light the candles on the wreath together each time you gather as a group during Advent. (All readings)

Second Sunday of Advent

Scripture Readings (5)

- ❖ Isa. 40:1–5,9–11
- ❖ Ps. 85:9–10,11–12,13–14
- ❖ 2 Pet. 3:8–14
- ❖ Mark 1:1–8

God's Word

A major theme of the Scripture readings is "A call for change."

The first reading is a great comfort to people who suffer oppression in exile. It sounds like a newspaper vendor crying out, "Extra! Extra! Read all about it." The prophet's message—to prepare a way for the Lord—strongly suggests that something new is about to begin, that a great change is going to take place. The images of God, for whom the way is to be prepared, are contrasting ones—a powerful God with strong arms, but also a gentle comforter who speaks tenderly and holds lambs in those arms.

The psalm celebrates the kindness of God who comes with peace and justice for those who hear and fear God. The psalm captures both the frustration and the hope of God's people. They are hopeful that God will bring justice and peace, yet impatient at having to wait for that to happen.

The Second Letter of Peter echoes Isaiah's announcement that the Lord is coming and that a radical change will take place. The change will result in a new heaven and a new earth. Likewise, the people who await the Lord's coming must change—repent and try to live without stain or defilement, and at peace in the Lord's sight. Waiting in this manner is not a waste of time. God will decide when all is ready for the Lord's Second Coming, and people can use the time to make things right between themselves and God.

The first words of the Gospel of Mark are from the Isaiah passage for this Sunday. These words are used to introduce John the Baptist, who was sent to prepare the way for the coming of Jesus. John sees repentance and the forgiveness of sins as the way to wait and get ready for the coming of Jesus. He baptizes those who believe him, as a sign of a new birth coming in Jesus.

John's call—the call of Advent—is a call to change, a call to conversion, a call to wait patiently and confidently for the coming of the Lord.

Themes for Teens   The following themes from the Scriptures relate to the lives of teens:
- Prepare the way of the Lord.
- Justice and peace walk with God.
- Repent and be saved.
- One who is more powerful will follow.
- Jesus is the Good News.

Our Response

Activity   ## Making a List, Checking It Twice

This activity is keyed to the readings as a whole. It asks the teens to set their priorities for Advent and urges them to make a place in the hustle and bustle of commercial Christmas preparations to reflect on the spiritual messages of the season.

Ask the young people to make a list of all the things they need to do to get ready for Christmas. They can to do this individually or as a group.

Next, tell them to make another list of things they will do during Advent to prepare for the coming of the Lord.

Distribute Advent calendars to the teens or have them each make one. Direct them to write in the things they are going to do during Advent to prepare for the coming of the Lord.

Activity Ideas   The following activity ideas also relate to the Scripture readings. You may want to read the passage(s) indicated as part of the activity.

- Encourage the young people to schedule some quiet time into every day of Advent. Explain that quiet time can be the desert time referred to in the Scriptures as a time to listen to God's voice. Have them pose these questions to themselves: How is God calling me? How is God hoping to change my heart? (All readings)

- Turn your group into headline writers for this activity. Have them write headlines for tomorrow's newspaper, announcing a world where
    - kindness and truth shall meet,
      justice and peace shall kiss,
      truth shall spring out of the earth,
      justice shall look down from heaven.

(Ps. 85:9–10,11–12,13–14)

- Direct the teens to list in their journal the images of God found in the first reading. Have them note the image of God they most relate to at this time in their life. Then ask them to describe in their journal how this image speaks to them. Finally, have them write a prayer, using their chosen image to address God. (Isa. 40:1–5,9–11)

- Discuss how the following quote by Pope Paul VI relates to today's readings: "'If you want peace, work for justice'" (quoted in Hamma, ed., *A Catechumen's Lectionary*, p. 19). Then send the teens out on a scavenger hunt to collect quotes on peace and justice. Create a collage on a bulletin board to help raise community awareness of the need to work for justice. (All readings)

Third Sunday of Advent

Scripture Readings
(8)

- ❖ Isa. 61:1–2,10–11
- ❖ Luke 1:46–48,49–50,53–54
- ❖ 1 Thess. 5:16–24
- ❖ John 1:6–8,19–28

God's Word

A major theme of the Scripture readings is "Prepare for Jesus, the light of the world."

Isaiah is filled with the Spirit and anointed by God to announce and prepare for the coming of the Lord. As such he is called to service—to reach out to the poor, the brokenhearted, the prisoner. He sees God making justice grow like plants in a garden. Christians interpret this text as a description of Jesus' role.

The responsorial psalm is not from the Psalms at all, but is taken from Luke's Gospel, in which Mary, having conceived Jesus by the power of the Spirit, expresses the greatness that has come to her in being anointed by God to give birth to the Son of God.

The passage from the First Letter to the Thessalonians is exceptionally upbeat. The Second Coming of the Lord will be a great day for those who are open to the Spirit and remain faithful to God.

In the Gospel reading, John the Baptist makes it clear that his role is to prepare for the coming of Jesus, the light of the world. John isn't the light. His job is to reflect the light of Jesus. He is only a voice crying out in the desert that the Lord is coming.

Themes for Teens

The following themes from the Scriptures relate to the lives of teens:
- Bring glad tidings to the poor.
- God has done great things for us.
- Rejoice always!
- Give the Spirit some room.
- Jesus is the light of the world.

Our Response

Activity

The Magnificat

This activity is keyed to the Psalm. It introduces the young people to the Magnificat, one of the beautiful traditional prayers of the church.

Have the teens pray the Magnificat. Give them a copy of the version of the Magnificat found below. Encourage them to take it home and pray it every night during the remaining days of Advent, asking Mary to give them the courage to approach God with humility and an openness to God's will and spirit in their lives.

The Magnificat

Left: My soul proclaims the greatness of the Lord,
my spirit rejoices in God, my savior,
Right: For God has looked upon the handmaid's lowliness;
behold, from now on all ages shall call me blessed.

Left: The mighty one has done great things for me,
and holy is God's name.
Right: God's mercy is from age to age
to those who fear God.

Left: God has shown might with his arm,
dispersing the arrogant of mind and heart.
Right: God has thrown down rulers from their thrones
but lifted up the lowly.

Left: God has filled the hungry with good things;
the rich are sent away empty.
Right: God has helped the servant Israel,
remembering mercy,

Left: according to God's promise to our fathers,
to Abraham and his descendants forever.

(Adapted from *Christian Prayer: The Liturgy of the Hours*
[New York: Catholic Book Publishing Co., 1976], p. 696)

Activity Ideas

The following activity ideas also relate to the Scripture readings. You may want to read the passage(s) indicated as part of the activity.

- Help the younger children in your parish community plant a "garden" of peace and justice. You can plant it on a large bulletin board in your parish center. They can make evergreen trees, holly bushes, wreaths, and poinsettias out of construction paper. Before the children plant (paste) their creations in the garden, ask them to write one way they will try to be more peaceful or just toward others. (Isa. 61:1–2,10–11)

- Ask the young people to think of some of the many blessings God has showered on them. Start a class book of blessings by asking each teen to write down at least one way God has blessed her or him in the past week. (Luke 1:46–48,49–50,53–54)

- Ask the teens to name the voices that compete for their attention this time of year. Do some of the voices yell "Buy, buy, buy"? Have them compare and contrast these commercial holiday voices with the voices they hear in today's Scripture readings. Discuss how we can tune out the wrong voices and tune in the voices of the Scriptures. (John 1:6–8,19–28)

- First, pose the following question to your group:
  ○ Are you tired of waiting for Christmas to come?
  Then mention that Advent is a season of waiting, but no one likes to wait. Acknowledge that although it is hard to be patient, Paul gives us ideas of what to do while we are waiting. He tells us to rejoice, pray, and give thanks. Invite the teens to alternate the following prayer starters in their journal during the remaining days of Advent:
  ○ Lord, I rejoice in your . . .
  ○ Lord, I pray for . . .
  ○ Lord, thank you for . . .

(1 Thess. 5:16–24)

Fourth Sunday of Advent

Scripture Readings (11)

- ❖ 2 Sam. 7:1–5,8–11,16
- ❖ Ps. 89:2–3,4–5,27,29
- ❖ Rom. 16:25–27
- ❖ Luke 1:26–38

God's Word

A major theme of the Scripture readings is "Say yes to God!"

In the first reading, King David wants to build a house (temple) for the Lord. But through Nathan, David learns that God doesn't want him to construct a building at all. Rather, God will build David's house—first in the people of a line of kings descending from David, and then in the person of Jesus.

Within the context of the readings for this Sunday, the psalm celebrates the fulfillment of the promise God made to David concerning the everlasting King, Jesus, that will come from his lineage.

Paul tells the Romans that all that has come true in the person of Jesus was promised in the early teachings of the prophets. Jesus' coming fulfills God's early promises to the people. What once was a mystery is made clear for all to see, understand, and believe.

The Gospel reading relates how Mary came to know she would be the mother of God. Mary is amazed at what the angel has to tell her. She is to conceive by the Holy Spirit, bear God's son, and name the child Jesus. Mary questions the angel's message. She knows the facts of life, but the angel answers that all things are possible with God. Mary turns herself over to the will of God, and her yes makes our salvation possible. As Advent draws to a close, let us join with Mary and speak to God, "Let it be done to me as you say."

Themes for Teens

The following themes from the Scriptures relate to the lives of teens:
- Let God dwell in you.
- God's mystery is revealed.
- Nothing is impossible with God.
- Say yes to God.
- God's will be done.

Our Response

Activity

Say Yes to God!

This activity is keyed to the Gospel reading. It allows the young people to hear the faith stories of those who have chosen to become Catholic and invites them to begin to say yes to their faith with their own heart.

Invite some neophytes—newly baptized Catholics—to give short witness talks to your group. Ask them to talk on the theme "Why I said yes to God."

Then ask the young people to reflect on their reasons for being Catholic. Lead a discussion, using questions like these:
- Are you Catholic because your parents are Catholic?
- In what ways do you practice your faith and share your faith with others?
- Have you made your own decision to be a Catholic? Was there a particular time or event when you did this?

On a thin strip of colored construction paper, ask each person to write one way that he or she can say yes to God. Link the strips together into a paper chain. Talk about how joining together in a community of faith helps us to say yes to God and become a house in which God dwells. Decorate a parish or school Christmas tree with your paper chain.

Activity Ideas

The following activity ideas also relate to the Scripture readings. You may want to read the passage(s) indicated as part of the activity.

- In a format similar to the prayers of intercession at Mass, pray for some of the seemingly impossible situations that the teens are involved in or know about. Let the response to the prayers be, "Nothing is impossible with God." (Luke 1:26–38)

- Instead of Christmas cards, have the young people send Advent cards—birth announcements for Jesus. Birth announcements can be found at most gift shops or discount stores. Suggest that the young people include a copy of the Magnificat or Hail Mary so that the recipients can pray to Mary as part of their preparation for the coming of Jesus at Christmas. (All readings)

- Have the teens hold a baby shower for Jesus and invite members of the parish or school community. Give all the gifts they collect to a home for unwed mothers or a shelter for battered women. (Luke 1:26–38)

- Ask the teens to do some research on Catholic devotions to Mary. Include a sharing time when they can talk about prayers, the rosary, pilgrimages to Lourdes, May processions, and other ways we ask Mary to intercede for us with her Son, Jesus. If the young people are unfamiliar with these prayers, you may want to teach them how to pray the rosary or say the Hail Mary. (Luke 1:26–38)

Christmas

Sunday in the Octave of Christmas (Holy Family)

Scripture Readings (17)

- ❖ Sir. 3:2–6,12–14
- ❖ Ps. 128:1–2,3,4–5
- ❖ Col. 3:12–21
- ❖ Luke 2:22–40

God's Word

A major theme of the Scripture readings is "Love rooted in family."

The reading from Sirach expands on the commandment to honor one's father and mother. Although the word *respect* is not used directly, honor, reverence, comfort, kindness, and consideration all add up to respect. The reading informs us that God holds parents in a special place of honor. Treating parents the way God prescribes will lead to riches, children, a long life, atonement, and many other good things. Obedience to parents is equated with obedience to God.

The psalm seems directed at the head of the family, suggesting that if the head of the family fears the Lord and walks in the ways of God, good things will come to the family. Fear of the Lord does not mean that God is unapproachable or that we should be frightened of God. It means that we should treat God with reverence and respect as our Creator and Savior.

The passage from Colossians, in effect, is the blueprint for living as a Christian family. It gives specific instructions for how Christians and Christian families are to act toward one another and toward God. In general, the passage calls us to put on the love of Christ and allow that love to guide all our actions.

The Gospel reading chronicles the journey of Mary, Joseph, and Jesus to the Temple in Jerusalem. Mary and Joseph go to acknowledge Jesus as a gift from God and to present Jesus to God in return. The Holy Family encounters Simeon, a pious man, and Anna, a prophet, who both recognize Jesus for who he really is. Simeon knows Jesus is the fulfillment of God's Word, and Anna recognizes Jesus as the one who will deliver Israel. But this joy is tempered by words of caution for Mary. Anna tells Mary that Mary will pay a price for being the mother of one with such an important destiny, that she will suffer great sadness. This caution alludes to the way Jesus will meet his death—on the cross.

Themes for Teens

The following themes from the Scriptures relate to the lives of teens:

- Respect your parents.
- Walk in God's ways.
- Put on love.
- Do all in God's name.
- Love is rooted in family.

Our Response

Activity   Celebrate Family

This activity is keyed to the readings as a whole. Youth groups and classes do not usually meet formally during this time of year. However, it is a perfect time for special events and family gatherings, because many people come home for the holidays. Here are some activities your youth community might use to honor and celebrate family during the week between Christmas and New Year's Day. You may want to plan one of these or a combination of a few of them.

Family Breakfast

Ask the teens to invite their parents or entire immediate family to a family breakfast. Have the teens set and decorate the tables, cook the meal, and wait on tables.

Family Prayer Book

Direct the teens to place a book with blank, ruled pages on a small stand in the commons of your parish. Have them prepare an accompanying poster with an invitation to families to write prayers of petition for family members who need prayers right now. Include an invitation to the entire community to remember these intentions in their prayers during the week.

Not Home for the Holidays

Ask the young people to prepare "Taste of Home" gift packages for family members who cannot come home for the holidays. Include homemade food, an audiocassette or video of recorded greetings, and a small booklet of original Christmas prayers.

Prayer Families

Invite the teens to swap prayer families with one another for the holidays. Each family gets the name of another family to remember in their prayers.

Family Ornament

Invite everyone in your group to lead their family in making a Christmas ornament that symbolizes their family. Have them bring the ornament to the next meeting and share its meaning with the group. The ornaments can then be used to decorate your worship space.

Activity Ideas

The following activity ideas also relate to the Scripture readings. You may want to read the passage(s) indicated as part of the activity.

- Invite the young people to share some of the ways their family traditionally celebrates Christmas. Focus on those that deepen the spiritual aspect of the season. For example, lighting the Advent wreath each week as a family, setting a place for the Christ child at Christmas Eve dinner, and so on. Encourage the teens to interview extended family members about ethnic traditions to discover how these traditions deepen faith and bind the family together. (All readings)

- Suggest that the teens share today's second reading with their family and have them list all the qualities that signify a good Christian. Then direct the teens to invite their family members to affirm one another for the gifts and talents they bring to the family. They can start with the qualities of a good Christian and add other relevant qualities. (Col. 3:12–21)

- Tell the young people to write a short note of affirmation to each member of their family, thanking that person for the nonmaterial gifts she or he gives them all year long, not just at Christmas. (Col. 3:12–21)

- Have each teen wrap a small box with white paper and decorate it with red and green ribbon or yarn. Direct them to write on the package, with green and red markers, ideas for remembering and honoring their family members at times other than Christmas. Invite them to share their ideas with the rest of the group. (All readings)

- Ask the teens to glue to a sheet of paper in their journal a picture of their family and a Christmas card picture of the Holy Family—Jesus, Mary, and Joseph. Then direct them to write a response to this question: What do your family and the Holy Family share in common? (Luke 2:22–40)

Second Sunday After Christmas

Scripture Readings (19)

- ❖ Sir. 24:1–4,8–12
- ❖ Ps. 147:12–13,14–15,19–20
- ❖ Eph. 1:3–6,15–18
- ❖ John 1:1–18

God's Word

A major theme of the Scripture readings is "The Word became flesh."

The reading from Sirach gives wisdom a voice. Wisdom says that she comes from the mouth of God and has been given a special place in the heavens to dwell. She does not remain in the heavens, but comes down to dwell in the people as the word of God.

The psalm celebrates the word of God sent to live among us. The word of God is not an abstract concept; it is the intimate presence of God that is part of the fabric of human life. The psalm points toward the great mystery of Jesus coming as the incarnate Word of God.

The second reading shows us that Jesus, the incarnate Word of God, is the center of God's plan for our salvation. The Letter to the Ephesians talks about how God sent Jesus to bring blessings firsthand and that in union with Jesus, people become adopted children of God. The author celebrates the Ephesian community's faith in Jesus. He prays for the gift of wisdom so that they will learn more about God, through Jesus, and grow closer to God.

The Gospel reading from John is the definitive statement about Jesus as the Word of God made flesh. We learn that the word of God was present in the beginning with the Creator, and, in time, became flesh in Jesus, the life and light for all. Jesus is the real light that came into the world and is a gift meant to be shared by all.

Themes for Teens   The following themes from the Scriptures relate to the lives of teens:
- Jesus is the Word of God.
- God grant us wisdom.
- The Word is God.
- Jesus is the Light of the World.
- The Word became flesh.

Our Response

Activity   Word and Light

This prayer service is keyed to the Gospel reading. It asks the young people to reflect on the powerful symbols of light and the Word and how these symbols can enlighten us about Jesus.

Before you begin this prayer service, give each teen a Bible and a taper candle.

Begin by proclaiming today's readings as you would during the liturgy of the word. In place of the homily, gather the teens in groups of four to "break open the Word" and share their own reflections on what the Gospel means to them. When they are finished, ask them to reflect quietly on the question, How will you share the Word by your life?

Next, as the leader, light one candle and sing, "The light of Christ has come into the world; the light of Christ has come into the world." ("The Light of Christ," by Donald Fishal, music available in *Songs of Praise Combined Edition* [Ann Arbor, MI: Servant Book Express], no. 52). Pass the light to a person near you and ask that person to join in singing the refrain. Continue passing the light. As each person's candle is lit, that person joins in the singing, so that the light and the singing continue to grow. When all the candles are lit, end the refrain and ask the teens to reflect quietly on the question, How will you share the light by your life?

Ask the teens to leave the prayer space in a single-file procession of light.

Activity Ideas   The following activity ideas also relate to the Scripture readings. You may want to read the passage(s) indicated as part of the activity.

- If some of the teens in your group do not own a Bible, consider giving each of them one as a Christmas present. If the teens in your group are fortunate enough to have their own Bible, consider a fund-raiser to purchase Bibles for teens in disadvantaged schools or parishes. (All readings)

- As a craft project, have the teens make and decorate Bible bookmarks that say, "Jesus is the Word of God." Direct them to distribute the bookmarks in the parish or school community as part of a campaign to raise awareness about the importance of reading the Scriptures. (All readings)

- Encourage the teens to identify some of the powerful symbols found in today's readings. Ask them what the symbols of word and light reveal about Jesus. Tell each teen to bring a Christmas symbol from home and to share how it might serve to deepen faith. Here are some examples:
  - A star reminds me of the star the Magi followed to find Jesus and of how we need to search for Jesus in our own life.
  - A Christmas tree reminds us that God's love for us is ever-green, everlasting.
  - A wreath, shaped in a circle, tells us that God's love has no beginning and no end. It is eternal.

(All readings)

Epiphany Sunday

Scripture Readings (20)

❖ Isa. 60:1–6
❖ Ps. 72:1–2,7–8,10–11,12–13
❖ Eph. 3:2–3,5–6
❖ Matt. 2:1–12

God's Word

A major theme of the Scripture readings is "Jesus comes for all."

The first reading, like last week's readings, foreshadows the coming of Jesus as the Light of the World. The author uses imagery of the rising and setting sun to portray God's favor and disfavor. Light is used to show when God is happy, or glad. Darkness usually means the people are in trouble. We are told to raise our head, open our eyes, and see how different the world looks when lit by the radiance of God.

The psalm echoes the last part of the first reading—that God is God for many nations, not just the people of Israel. Today, the birth of Jesus is celebrated all over the world by people of different races, ages, and economic means. The psalm reads as a tribute to a king—a king who is just and who has a place for afflicted people in the Kingdom.

The passage from the Letter to the Ephesians, like the first reading and the psalm, states that the Gospel is not meant for just one select group of people, but is to be shared with all. The secret (mystery) that the author talks about is, in fact, that the Kingdom of God is for everyone. The Gospel is not to be kept quiet. We must proclaim it from the rooftops.

Matthew's Gospel passage relates the story of the astrologers (often referred to as kings or magi) who follow a star to find the newborn Jesus, who they heard was the Messiah. These kings are not Jews, but they come with gifts to pay homage to Jesus, who was born for all, not just for one group. The kings are not only on a physical journey, they are on a spiritual journey as well. They do not really know where they are going, but they just keep following the star and trusting that God will get them there. Like the kings, we are also on a spiritual journey, and we can trust that God will show us the way to Jesus.

Themes for Teens

The following themes from the Scriptures relate to the lives of teens:
- Walk in the light.
- In God's eyes, we are all equal.
- We are one in Christ.
- We are to proclaim the Gospel, not keep it quiet.
- Honor Jesus with your gifts.

Our Response

Activity

Ecumenical Pilgrimage

This activity is keyed to the readings as a whole. It encourages the teens to see the wider faith community beyond their own church and to raise their awareness of the need to reach out to and welcome people of different faiths.

Take the young people on a pilgrimage to several neighboring churches and synagogues. If they are not in walking distance, arrange a car caravan. At each stop, ask some of the people of the community to share with the young people how they celebrate Christmas or Hanukkah. Your teens can share some of their traditions as well. Offer a prayer at each site for cooperation of people of all faiths.

Activity Ideas

The following activity ideas also relate to the Scripture readings. You may want to read the passage(s) indicated as part of the activity.

- Invite the teens to honor the Christ child by reaching out to children in their community. Have them collect gifts for poor children, volunteer to baby-sit in the parish nursery during liturgies, read stories to children in the hospital, or buy snacks to give to children at an area soup kitchen. (Matt. 2:1–12)

- Ask the young people to respond to the following question in their journal: If you could bring one gift to the Christ child, what would it be? Why? (Matt. 2:1–12)

- Cut out magazine pictures of people of different races, ages, nationalities, or economic status. Direct the teens to talk about the person(s) in each picture based on appearances alone. Consider the danger of stereotypes and how they often lead to discrimination. Discuss how your youth community welcomes others who are different and how you might be even more welcoming. Explore ways to fight discrimination in the church and in the world. (Isa. 60:1–6; Eph. 3:2–3,5–6)

- Note that Christmas is not the end of the journey, that we—like the astrologers—need to set out on a spiritual journey. Ask the teens to brainstorm concrete ways they can keep the spirit of Christmas alive through the coming months. (Matt. 2:1–12)

Baptism of the Lord Sunday

Scripture Readings (21)

- ❖ Isa. 42:1–4,6–7
- ❖ Ps. 29:1–2,3–4,3,9–10
- ❖ Acts 10:34–38
- ❖ Mark 1:7–11

God's Word

A major theme of the Scripture readings is "Born to serve the world."

The reading from Isaiah carries a promise that God will send a servant to establish justice on the earth. The Servant Savior is quiet and gentle, does not make much noise, but is also powerful, bringing justice to the entire world. This reading foreshadows Jesus—a servant empowered by God to bring justice, a light for all nations who will open the eyes of the blind and save those who are imprisoned by injustice.

The psalm bears a blessing of peace. Unlike the quiet servant in the first reading, here God's voice thunders over all the waters. We are called to praise and honor this mighty God. Our reward for our reverence will be a blessing of peace.

The reading from Acts makes it clear that the Good News about Jesus is for all people to hear, that Jesus Christ is the Lord of all, and that the goodness of peace is God's desire and gift for all.

The passage from Mark's Gospel tells of Jesus' baptism by John. Jesus' baptism marks the beginning of his mission to preach about repentance and the arrival of God's Kingdom. The imagery and God's words confirm that Jesus is truly the servant that God has promised to send into the world to bring justice and peace to all. John's work of preparing the way is now done. The one who follows him, and who is more powerful than he, is now present.

Themes for Teens   The following themes from the Scriptures relate to the lives of teens:
- Jesus is a light to all nations.
- The Good News does not discriminate.
- God keeps promises.
- Jesus is God's Son.
- Baptism calls us to serve.

Our Response

Activity   Renewal of Baptismal Promises

This activity is keyed to the Gospel reading. It invites the teens to remember and reaffirm the promises made for them by others when they were baptized and serves as a reminder of their baptismal call to serve.

Leader: Do you reject sin so as to live in the freedom of God's children?
All: I do.

Leader: Do you reject the glamour of evil, and refuse to be mastered by sin?
All: I do.

Leader: Do you reject Satan, father of sin and prince of darkness?
All: I do.

Leader: Do you believe in God, the Father almighty, creator of heaven and earth?
All: I do.

Leader: Do you believe in Jesus Christ, his only Son, our Lord, who was born of the Virgin Mary, was crucified, died, and was buried, rose from the dead, and is now seated at the right hand of the Father?
All: I do.

Leader: Do you believe in the Holy Spirit, the holy catholic Church, the communion of saints, the forgiveness of sins, the resurrection of the body, and life everlasting?
All: I do.

Leader: This is our faith. This is the faith of the Church. We are proud to profess it, in Christ Jesus our Lord.
All: Amen.

(*Rites of the Catholic Church,* vol. 1, pp. 401–402)

Activity Ideas

The following activity ideas also relate to the Scripture readings. You may want to read the passage(s) indicated as part of the activity.

- If children in your parish are being baptized on this day or during the holidays, plan for your group to attend at least one baptism and later discuss the group members' reactions to the event. Also suggest that the teens find out about their own baptism by asking their parents to describe it and to explain why they made the decision to have their child baptized Catholic. (Mark 1:7–11)

- Invite an adult who was baptized at the previous Easter Vigil to give a witness talk to the group about his or her decision to become a Catholic and what the experience of being baptized meant. (Mark 1:7–11)

- Have the teens explore the symbols connected with baptism. Consider holding this discussion around your parish's baptismal font. Have a candle, a white garment, and some oil nearby. Ask the teens what they think each of these elements symbolizes. Explain where and how these elements are used in the Rite of Baptism. (Mark 1:7–11)

- Note that every call requires a response and that Jesus responded to his baptismal call to serve. Then direct the teens to reflect on how they are presently responding to their baptismal call and how they plan to respond to it in the future. (All readings)

Lent

First Sunday of Lent

Scripture Readings (23)

- ❖ Gen. 9:8–15
- ❖ Ps. 25:4–5,6–7,8–9
- ❖ 1 Pet. 3:18–22
- ❖ Mark 1:12–15

God's Word

A major theme of the Scripture readings is "God's promise fulfilled."

In chapter 9 of Genesis, we find a story about Noah, his family, and the animals getting off the ark to view a wonderful rainbow in the sky. God promises to never again destroy the earth with a great flood. As a sign of a pledge to keep this promise, God places a rainbow in the sky for all to see.

The responsorial psalm says that following the ways of the Lord is the people's part of the terms of the covenant. However, the people need help in carrying out this commitment. The psalmist asks God to be a teacher and a guide, and to be compassionate and kind when we stumble on our way along the right path.

The second reading, from First Peter, links the story about the covenant made with Noah in the first reading with the covenant fulfilled in Jesus Christ. Water is a key image here. In the Noah story, water was both a means of destruction as well as a means of escape. This reading speaks of the waters of baptism, which were prefigured in the flood, as the means of salvation for those who believe.

This short Gospel reading does not give much detail about Jesus' forty-day stay in the desert. The important point is that it marked the beginning of Jesus' mission to fulfill the promise made by God to save humankind. Jesus comes back from the desert with a sense of urgency; he is renewed and eager to get his message across—repent and believe!

We have begun the season of Lent, a time to repent and renew our belief in God's promise.

Themes for Teens

The following themes from the Scriptures relate to the lives of teens:
- God keeps promises.
- God is our teacher and guide.
- The waters will save us.
- Leave the devil in the desert.
- Repent and hear the Good News.

Our Response

Activity — God's Good News

This creative activity is keyed to all the readings. It challenges the young people to share the Good News of Jesus by creating their own newspaper. Introduce the activity in the following way:

> When Jesus left the desert, he began preaching and teaching the message to repent and believe in the Good News. Your newspaper has been assigned to follow this great man, Jesus. Beginning with today's readings, your task is to publish a newspaper that spreads the Good News of Jesus.

Divide the group into teams. Ask each team to name its newspaper. Some examples are the *Good News Gazette* or the *Promise Times*.

Next, direct the teams to write stories, take photos, and edit and design the pages of their newspaper. Offer the following as some possible features:

- Take the first reading about Noah and rewrite it as a news story. Include tips on keeping the covenant.
- Develop an advice column on ways to repent and be saved.
- Write up the encounter of Jesus and the devil as a sports story.
- Write a feature on 1001 ways water is used in the Scriptures.

If you have access to a desktop publishing system, help the teens put their newspapers together and publish them as a supplement to your parish newsletter or school newspaper.

Activity Ideas

The following activity ideas also relate to the Scripture readings. You may want to read the passage(s) indicated as part of the activity.

- A rainbow appears in today's first reading as a sign of God's covenant with us. Direct the teens to search the Hebrew Scriptures for ways the writers used signs from nature to describe their relationship with God. Then have the young people search the Christian Testament for ways Jesus used nature as a way to teach the Good News. (Gen. 9:8–15)

- Make a big banner with a rainbow on it, to place on a wall in your meeting space. Write on the top, "God keeps promises." Ask the young people to write on the banner, using colored markers that match the colors of the rainbow, some of the many ways God keeps promises to them and to your group. (All readings)

- Take your group outdoors (weather permitting) to an ocean, lake, river, or stream. Share today's readings and discuss the meaning of water in these passages. End with a short prayer that asks the teens to dip their fingers in the water and make the sign of the cross to mark Lent as a time to start following the cross of Jesus. (All readings)

- Note that each verse of the psalm begins with a different letter of the alphabet. Have the teens write those letters vertically down the left margin of a sheet of paper. Form small groups and challenge them to write one-line modern prayers in which each prayer starts with the first letter of each verse of the psalm. (Ps. 25:4–5,6–7,8–9)

Second Sunday of Lent

Scripture Readings (26)

- ❖ Gen. 22:1–2,9,10–13,15–18
- ❖ Ps. 116:10,15,16–17,18–19
- ❖ Rom. 8:31–34
- ❖ Mark 9:2–10

God's Word

A major theme of the Scripture readings is "Tests of faith."

God really put Abraham to a tough test. What can be more precious to a parent than her or his own child? Asking Abraham to sacrifice his son is seen by Christians as a foreshadowing of what God will do in sacrificing Jesus to rescue us from eternal death. Abraham set about doing what God required, getting everything ready for the sacrifice. But what a relief it must have been when the Lord's messenger stopped the sacrifice.

The psalm reads as though it could have been written by Abraham. The psalmist still believes in God despite all that he was asked to give up. Even in the midst of great trial, the author's faith is not diminished.

The reading from Romans allows us to see that God didn't ask Abraham to do anything God wasn't willing to do. What other proof should we need of God's love than the sacrifice of God's Son?

In Mark's Gospel, Jesus takes a few of his disciples for a hike up a mountain. Elijah and Moses show up to talk with Jesus. They represent the Law and the prophets, which previously conveyed the promises of God. Jesus is the fulfillment of both. The voice of God makes it clear who Jesus is, "'This is my Son, my beloved. Listen to him.'" Jesus asks the disciples to keep secret what they just saw and heard, what they know will not be revealed to all until after Jesus' Resurrection.

Coming down from the mountain, Jesus talks about his death. The disciples do not understand that to share in God's glory is to share in Jesus' suffering and death.

Themes for Teens

The following themes from the Scriptures relate to the lives of teens:
- I'm ready, God!
- Give all to God.
- God is on our side.
- Listen to Jesus.
- Say yes to God.

Our Response

Activity   Lenten Sculpture

This discussion and mime activity is keyed to the readings as a whole. It asks the young people to reflect on the meaning of Lent and challenges them to think of sacrifice as more than just giving up little things for a few weeks.

Divide the teens into small groups and give each group a piece of paper and some pencils. Ask the groups to write the word *Lent* across the top of the paper and to brainstorm at least fifteen words that come to mind when they think of Lent.

Invite each group of teens to create human sculptures about what Lent means to them. For example, if a group has eight members, ask each one to choose a word from the group list and figure out a way to express it using only his or her body and without using any spoken words. Each word and action will be added together with the rest to form one group tableau that represents Lent.

Give each group a separate place to work on its human sculptures. Allow the teens 20 minutes to conceive and practice their sculptures. Then have them share their sculptures with everyone.

Afterward, give the teens some quiet time to ponder the following questions. Then discuss the questions as a group:
- What did you learn about Lent from this activity?
- How is Lent much more than giving up candy bars for forty days?
- What sacrifices can you make for God during Lent?
- What sacrifices can you make for others during Lent?

Activity Ideas   The following activity ideas also relate to the Scripture readings. You may want to read the passage(s) indicated as part of the activity.

- Plan a prayer service based on the prescription for following God that is found in the psalm: Offer service, make sacrifices, call God's name. (Ps. 116:10,15,16–17,18–19)

- Ask the question, How well do we listen to God? Then direct the teens to search the Scriptures for some examples of things Jesus said that we should listen to. Ask each group to pick one and then act out a skit, in the context of modern times, showing how we can listen to the words of Jesus and put them into action. (Mark 9:2–10)

- As the teens arrive for your meeting or class this week, do something dramatic at the beginning to get their attention. Some ideas: Pop a balloon, blow a trumpet, use a bullhorn, arrive in an unusual costume. Talk about what God did to get the Apostles' attention during the Transfiguration of Jesus. Ask the teens what God does to get their attention and what they can do to pay better attention to God? (Mark 9:2–10)

- Tell the teens to divide one page in their journal in half vertically. On one side, have them make a list of at least ten of their wants, and on the other side, a list of what they think God wants for them. Ask them to compare the lists. Encourage them to consider what they must do to put what God wants before what they want, and how they will tackle this effort during Lent. (All readings)

Third Sunday of Lent

**Scripture Readings
(29)**
- ❖ Exod. 20:1–17
- ❖ Ps. 19:8,9,10,11
- ❖ 1 Cor. 1:22–25
- ❖ John 2:13–25

God's Word   A major theme of the Scripture readings is "Laws of love."

The passage from Exodus maps out the details of the Ten Commandments God gave to Moses to share with the people. The first three, written with extra detail, talk about how we should relate to God. The rest are a list of ways we should relate to others. They are God's laws of love, representing the people's obligations in the covenant with God. These laws are not suggestions. They demand that we treat God and others with love and respect. Jesus later condensed these ten into two—telling us to love God and our neighbor.

The psalmist finds God's laws to be sweeter than honey and more precious than gold. God's laws are praised as right, clear, perfect, and just, because they represent the people's part of the covenant made with God.

In First Corinthians, we hear how neither Greek philosophy nor Jewish signs (prophecies) could make sense of a crucified savior. Only the worst criminals were crucified. The people wanted a king as a savior. We also get a hint of just how far God will go, in Jesus, to be faithful to God's part of the covenant—to the point of death on the cross.

In the Gospel of John, Jesus gets fed up with the mockery of God and God's Commandments that is taking place through all the wheeling and dealing in the Temple. This usually gentle man knocks over tables, uses strong language, and drives out the money changers. Jesus demands the respect for God and God's designated house that the Commandments call for, even to the point of risking his life.

Jesus tells the people gathered that if they destroy the Temple of God he will rebuild it in three days. As usual, the disciples take Jesus literally. They know how long it takes to build a temple. What they don't realize is that Jesus is talking about the temple of his body, and his own death and Resurrection.

Themes for Teens   The following themes from the Scriptures relate to the lives of teens:
- Keep the commandments.
- God's word brings life.
- God is wiser than us.
- Keep God's space holy.
- Jesus is the sign of the times.

Our Response

Activity   ### From Don'ts to Do's

This discussion activity is keyed to the first reading. It helps the teens review the Ten Commandments and transform them from a list of things not to do into some strategies for living God's law of love in today's world.

Before sharing today's first reading, ask the young people to see if they can remember the Ten Commandments. As they call out the Commandments, write them on a large sheet of poster board or a chalkboard.

Ask one of the teens to read Exod. 20:1–17. Then divide them into small groups and direct them to rewrite the Ten Commandments in modern language, starting with "You shall" instead of "You shall not."

When the young people are finished, ask a spokesperson from each group to share its commandments. Consider posting them in your meeting space for the rest of Lent.

Activity Ideas   The following activity ideas also relate to the Scripture readings. You may want to read the passage(s) indicated as part of the activity.

- Watch the 40-minute video *The Ten Commandments for Teens* (formerly called *God's Game Plan*). The video is available from Liguori Publications. See page 133 for their address and phone number. Follow the video with a discussion on ways we can follow each of the commandments more closely. (Exod. 20:1–17; Ps. 19:8,9,10,11)

- Make copies of street signs you might find on any road, for example, *stop, one way, slippery when wet, signal ahead, curve in road, fork in road,* and *no U-turn.* Ask the teens to answer the following questions by using the signs as discussion starters:
  - Which sign describes how you walk with God right now in your life?
  - Which sign describes how you would like that relationship to change?
  - Which sign can guide us on our journey through Lent?

(1 Cor. 1:22–25)

Lent

- Instruct the teens to make their own signs of the times. Invite them to design bumper stickers, T-shirts, or buttons that promote God's laws of love. Have them use quotes from today's readings or others from the Scriptures. (All readings)

- Ask the teens how they think Jesus might react to the bingo games, church bazaars, flea markets, and the like that take place in Catholic parishes today. How are these activities similar to the Temple scene in the Gospel? How are they different? (John 2:13–25)

Fourth Sunday of Lent

Scripture Readings (29)

❖ 2 Chron. 36:14–17,19–23
❖ Ps. 137:1–2,3,4–5,6
❖ Eph. 2:4–10
❖ John 3:14–21

God's Word

A major theme of the Scripture readings is "Choose life and light."

The first reading describes what happens when people fail to follow the light of God's word. God gives them plenty of warnings and second chances, but instead of heeding the warnings and changing their ways, they make fun of the prophets sent to them. Their Temple and city are destroyed, and they are taken into captivity. Even so, God's mercy prevails, and after seventy years of exile, the people are released and the construction of a new Temple in Jerusalem begins.

The responsorial psalm is the cry of a people who regret their ways only after it is too late. After all they have is gone, they remember God. The exiles are teased by their captors. But the exiles won't sing; they have put away their harps. But they keep hoping to return to their homeland.

The passage from Ephesians highlights God's mercy. Despite all that people may do to turn away from God, God is always merciful. God's mercy is their salvation. Even though people do good works, they are not saved by them. They are saved by God's mercy, given as a gift in Jesus, delivered by the cross.

Jesus' speech after his conversation with Nicodemus sums up the heart of the Gospel message: God's love is so great that he sent his Son to save humankind. Jesus came into the world, says John, to save all who believe and to invite them to walk in the light. But we have a free will and we can choose darkness or the light that is Jesus.

Themes for Teens

The following themes from the Scriptures relate to the lives of teens:
- Never lose sight of God.
- Repent before it's too late.
- No one earns salvation.
- God's mercy gave us his Son.
- Choose light over darkness.

Our Response

Activity   A Sacrament Misunderstood

This activity is keyed to all the readings. Ask the teens to share what they know about the sacrament of reconciliation. Make sure to discuss the reason for celebrating the sacrament: to ask God's forgiveness, to be freed from the burden of sin, and to repair relationships with God and others.

Share with the teens this summary of a newspaper article:

> A recent article described an online service called The Confession Booth. Increased computer use and fascination with the Internet has given birth to online churches and now computer confession.
>
> The digital priest asks, "How long has it been since your last confession?" You type in the number of days or weeks. Then you fill out a checklist itemizing your sins. You even get your penance electronically.
>
> If that isn't enough, you can read other people's confessions on a Scroll of Sins. (McKee, "Cyber Confession," p. C2)

Discuss this question with the young people: How does this online "confession booth" defeat the purpose of the real meaning of the sacrament?

Give each group one of the three readings or psalms from today. Ask them to relate the readings to this article.

Close by encouraging the young people to celebrate the sacrament of reconciliation during the last few weeks before Easter.

Activity Ideas

The following activity ideas also relate to the Scripture readings. You may want to read the passage(s) indicated as part of the activity.

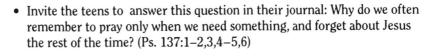

- Give each teen a small gift box. Inside the box, enclose a slip of paper containing the words, "You are saved." In pairs, ask the teens to share what they think the message means. Then read the Ephesians passage to the group. (Eph. 2:4–10)

- Invite the teens to answer this question in their journal: Why do we often remember to pray only when we need something, and forget about Jesus the rest of the time? (Ps. 137:1–2,3,4–5,6)

- Borrow a large heavy cross, preferably the size that would be used by an actor playing Jesus in living stations of the cross. Direct the teens one at a time to lift up the heavy cross and see how long they can hold it by themselves. Ask this question: What crosses do we carry in our life? Then tell everyone to get together to lift the cross. Ask this question: How do we need the help of others to help us carry our crosses? (All readings)

- Divide the young people into groups and ask them to brainstorm an example of a tough decision-making situation one of them might face. Then tell them to switch situations with another group. Have each group role-play its tough situation. As a large group, discuss situations in which teens are faced with choosing light versus choosing darkness. (John 3:14–21)

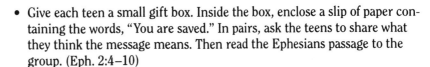

Fifth Sunday of Lent

Scripture Readings (35)

- ❖ Jer. 31:31–34
- ❖ Ps. 51:3–4,12–13,14–15
- ❖ Heb. 5:7–9
- ❖ John 12:20–33

God's Word

A major theme of the Scripture readings is "Death can bring life."

In Jeremiah, we hear God promise a new covenant to the people. However, the terms of the covenant—the Law—will not be written on stone tablets like the Ten Commandments. God will write them on human hearts, where obedience will be prompted by love rather than sanction. In the new covenant, people will come to a much closer relationship with God.

The psalmist asks God to wipe away from his heart all that keeps God and him apart. Grateful to be forgiven, the psalmist promises to share God's forgiveness and bring other sinners back to God. How good it is to know that although we cannot hope to remove transgressions from our heart, God will, in effect, create in us a clean heart.

In Hebrews, we learn that Jesus feared death and asked God for deliverance. His anguish shows that he suffered just as we do. Yet despite his fear, Jesus is an obedient son. God does not save Jesus from death, but brings him through death to Resurrection. His sacrifice is our salvation.

The Gospel reading continues the theme of the life-giving power of Jesus' death. At this point, Jesus realizes that the beginning of the end is upon him. In order to assure his disciples that his death will give rise to new life, Jesus uses the example of a grain of seed needing to be buried in the ground in order to sprout into new life. He also leaves us with a challenge: We who try to preserve our earthly life and are unwilling to die will lose our life; only those of us who give up our life will gain life.

At the same time, Jesus is weighed down by what is about to happen and says,

> "Yet what should I say—
> 'Father, save me from this hour?'
> But it was for this that I came to this hour.
> Father, glorify your name."

> And God answers,
> "I have glorified it,
> and will glorify it again."

God's plan for salvation unfolds in these readings. Jesus is about to die, like a seed that brings new life for all.

Themes for Teens

The following themes from the Scriptures relate to the lives of teens:

- Jesus is our new promise.
- Keep my heart clean, God.
- Jesus obeys the Father.
- We must die in order to live.
- The hour is near.

Our Response

Activity

Signs of Our Prayer

This prayer activity is keyed to all the readings. It invites the young people to reflect on the rich symbols found in the celebration of the seasons of Lent and Easter, and it helps them use these symbols as a springboard for prayer.

Place the following objects inspired by today's readings on a low table in the center of your prayer space: a washcloth, a shaft of wheat or some grains of wheat, and a picture or cut-out of a heart. Add other symbols of Lent and Easter: thorns, nails, palms, a purple cloth, a Bible, a cross, a paschal candle, a picture or symbol of a lamb, an egg, a lily, a butterfly.

Invite the teens to come forward, hold up one of the symbols, and share a prayer inspired by it. Here are some examples: "Dear God, please help me understand that I must die to my selfish ways in order to live with you" [wheat]. "Dear God, help me to recognize the promise of new life in all you create" [egg]. Do not limit the teens to the symbols on the table. They can choose other symbols that are important to them for their prayer.

A variation might be to ask the teens to bring their own Easter symbols from home to share with the group during this prayer time.

Activity Ideas

The following activity ideas also relate to the Scripture readings. You may want to read the passage(s) indicated as part of the activity.

- Tell the teens that the title of this activity is "Words of God Are Written on Your Heart." Give each teen a Bible and a name tag shaped like a heart. Ask them to locate their favorite Scripture passage and then write a significant part of it on their name tag, along with the Scripture citation (book, chapter, verse). Invite the teens to share with a partner their favorite passage and how God speaks to their heart through it. (Jer. 31:32–34)

- Invite the teens to pray today's psalm every morning when they awaken and every night before they go to sleep as a way of seeking God's forgiveness and help in preparing for the coming of Holy Week. (Ps. 51:3–4,12–13,14–15)

- Explore the theme "From death to life," using the seasons of the year. Ask the teens to identify a color or feeling they associate with the season of fall, winter, spring, or summer. Then direct them to write a prayer reflecting that color or feeling. Invite the teens to share with the whole group their color or feeling and the prayer they wrote. (All readings)

- Ask the teens to research some of the church's martyrs—contemporary or historic. Encourage the group members to look especially for the new growth that came from the martyr's death, as described in today's Gospel reading. At the next meeting, have them share their findings with the group. (John 12:20–33)

Palm Sunday

Scripture Readings (38)

- ❖ Isa. 50:4–7
- ❖ Ps. 22:8–9,17–18,19–20,23–24
- ❖ Phil. 2:6–11
- ❖ Mark 14:1–15,47

God's Word

A major theme of the Scripture readings is "The suffering of God's servants."

In the Book of Isaiah, we find a person who has been faithful and trusting toward God despite people who beat him and make fun of him. Like all prophets, this one suffers abuse in the name of God. He perseveres because he knows it is not a disgrace to serve God. This image of a suffering servant is later applied to Jesus Christ, who fulfills the role of a suffering servant of God.

The psalm continues the theme of hope despite persecution. The writer cries out, wondering why he is left alone to suffer. Here, too, the verses sound much like the suffering that Jesus endured on the cross, as recorded in the Gospel reading of the Passion. We read of pierced hands and of casting lots for garments. The verses present a sharp contrast between honor and humiliation—a lot like this Sunday's liturgy, with Jesus' triumphant procession of palms being followed by his death on the cross. Yet the psalmist continues to praise and give glory to God. Even in the depths of despair, we can trust in God.

In Philippians, we learn that Jesus did not hold on to his position as God. Instead, he humbled himself to be one of us and to die like one of us. But in accepting the humiliation of the cross, God exalted him and made him Lord of all.

In the reading of the Passion, we walk with Jesus through his suffering and death. It is draining, not so much because it is long, but more so because of the strong feelings it stirs within us.

Here is a brief outline of the chain of events: Jesus breaks the bread of his body and shares the wine of his blood at his last Passover meal with his friends. He struggles with his fate as he prays in the garden and then is abandoned by the disciples closest to him. One of them betrays Jesus to the authorities. Another one of his closest friends, Peter, saves himself by denying Jesus not once, but three times. Although earlier a crowd had followed Jesus through the streets with palms, singing his praises, now another crowd rejects him in favor of a criminal. When charged with being the King of the Jews, Jesus gives no defense and is sentenced to death. After Jesus has suffered terrible beatings, Simon of Cyrene carries Jesus' cross to the place of death. Jesus is nailed to the cross like a common criminal. After the agony of his death, he is buried in someone else's tomb.

Themes for Teens

The following themes from the Scriptures relate to the lives of teens:

- The Lord is my help.
- God will not abandon us.
- Jesus Christ is Lord.
- Jesus sacrificed himself for us.
- We stand by the cross.

Our Response

Activity

A Lenten Retreat

If your teens gather for only 45 minutes or an hour each week, set aside a half day for a retreat session to help draw Lent to a close and prepare them to experience Holy Week and Easter.

This activity is keyed to the Gospel reading. Divide the teens into small groups of six to eight. Give each group part of the text of today's reading of the Passion, for example, the Last Supper, the agony in the garden, the trial, and so on. Ask the groups to rewrite their assigned part from the point of view of a young bystander caught up in the events taking place.

Read the Passion according to the teens, with each group sharing the portion it wrote. Stop at the point were Jesus is crucified. Show the Crucifixion scene from the *Jesus of Nazareth* video, available from Bridgestone Multimedia. See page 133 for their address and phone number.

After watching the Crucifixion scene, encourage the teens to join with a partner and reflect on the Passion and describe some of their feelings to each other.

Give everyone a copy of the scriptural version of the Passion narrative to read on their own. Then ask them to write in their journal about one part of the narrative that really speaks to them.

For a closing prayer, ask the teens to sit in a circle and silently pass a crucifix from person to person. Invite them to offer a quiet prayer before passing the crucifix on to the next person.

At the end of your time together, invite the teens to participate fully in Holy Week services at their parish. Give each person a small wooden cross to wear as a remembrance of the retreat time together.

Activity Ideas

The following activity ideas also relate to the Scripture readings. You may want to read the passage(s) indicated as part of the activity.

- As your parish community prepares for Holy Week, ask if your group can be involved in the procession with palms, the reading of the Passion narrative, or the dramatization of Christ's Passion. The experience of communicating the Passion rather than just listening to it being read can be very powerful. (Mark 14:1–15,47)

- Invite the teens to choose a mantra from today's readings and pray it throughout Holy Week, until Easter. A mantra is a reverent, prayerful repetition of a short phrase in sync with one's breathing. Here are some possibilities from today's readings:
  - *Isa. 50:4–7.* The Lord God is my help.
  - *Ps. 22:8–9,17–18,19–20,23–24.* Be not far from me.
  - *Phil. 2: 6–11.* Jesus Christ is Lord.
  - *Mark 14:1–15,47.* Crucify him.

- A procession of palms precedes the eucharistic liturgy on Passion Sunday. It commemorates Jesus' triumphant entry into Jerusalem. Challenge your teens to plan this celebration as if Jesus were coming to their town or city today. For suggestion starters, ask:
  - Would you ask a marching band to play, decorate a float, arrange for TV coverage?
  - How would you greet Jesus today—with a song, a banner, three cheers, pom pons?

(Mark 14:1–15, 47)

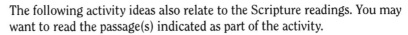

Lent

• After sharing the reading from Isaiah, pray for people who risk their life to stand up for truth and justice. Ask the young people to make their own holy cards with newspaper or magazine pictures of these modern saints on one side, and a prayer for justice on the other side. Invite them to share their holy cards with the group. (Isa. 50:4–7)

Easter

Easter Sunday

Scripture Readings
(43)

❖ Acts 10:34,37–43
❖ Ps. 118:1–2,16–17,22–23
❖ Col. 3:1–4
❖ John 20:1–9

God's Word

A major theme of the Scripture readings is "The tomb is empty."

Peter's speech from the Acts of the Apostles provides a short overview of Jesus' life, mission, and death. It reads like a news report of Jesus' life, from his roots in Nazareth to his Resurrection. The cross becomes a symbol of victory rather than a symbol of death. The people are called to be witnesses to this great legacy.

The psalm allows us to put away the melancholy of Lent and sing the alleluias of Easter. This is a great day, a day made by the Lord. A stone, once rejected by the builders, has become the stone the entire building rests on. Jesus, rejected by the leaders of Israel, is now risen and becomes the center of a whole new faith. Rejoice and be glad. We are saved by God and live triumphant over death.

In Colossians we are told that we, too, have been raised up with Christ. However, new life requires a new way of living. We are to set aside things of this earth and look to the things of above. We are to leave behind the old ways of death and participate in the new life of Easter.

The Gospel reading takes us right to the tomb on the first Easter morning. Day has hardly broken. Mary Magdalene goes to the tomb to find it empty. She runs to get the others. All they find are burial wrappings—no Jesus.

No one expects the Resurrection, despite all Jesus had foretold about it. They expect Jesus to still be lying in the tomb. Even when they have seen the empty tomb, their first thought is that someone has stolen his body.

To celebrate Easter is to remember that Jesus still lives and walks among us. The tomb is empty; Jesus is alive!

Themes for Teens

The following themes from the Scriptures relate to the lives of teens:
• If we believe, our sins are forgiven.
• Celebrate! Jesus lives!
• Alleluia!
• We rise again with Christ.
• The tomb is empty.

Our Response

Activity

A Story of Transformation

This activity is keyed to the Gospel reading. It is a story that helps teens recognize and reflect on the dramatic conversion experience of the Resurrection.

After sharing today's Gospel reading together, give each teen a copy of the story "Transformation to New Life," on page 50, to reflect on quietly by themselves.

"Transformation to New Life"

"What a great afternoon this is," thought the young boy. "Grandpa and me fishing all by ourselves." The two of them just talked and fished, and aimlessly drifted in a rowboat on a lake. The boy became restless . . . and he leaned over the side to look into the water. There, just beneath the surface, a bunch of water beetles were flitting around as if they were playing.

Suddenly one of the water beetles crawled up on an oar. When it got halfway up, it attached the talons of its legs to the wooden oar and died. The boy's curiosity was aroused and he interrupted his grandfather's nap to show him. They went back to fishing.

About three hours later, the boy looked down at the dead beetle. What he saw caused him to jump, almost tipping the boat. The beetle had dried up, and its shell started to crack open. Both the astonished grandfather and the boy watched silently at what unfolded before their eyes.

Something began to emerge from the opening: first long tentacles, then a head, then moist wings until, finally, a beautiful dragonfly fully emerged.

They both stared in awe. The dragonfly began to move its wings, slowly at first. Then it hovered gracefully over the water where the other water beetles were still flitting around. They didn't even recognize the dragonfly. They did not realize that it was the same beetle they had played with some three hours earlier.

The boy took his finger and nudged the dried-out shell of the beetle. It was like an empty tomb. (Cecil B. De Mille, quoted in Cavanaugh, *More Sower's Seeds*, pp. 41–42)

Consider inviting the teens to write reflections in their journal to cap off this activity.

Activity Ideas

The following activity ideas also relate to the Scripture readings. You may want to read the passage(s) indicated as part of the activity.

- After praying the responsorial psalm together, ask the young people to record in their journal some of their reasons for giving thanks today. (Ps. 118:1–2,16–17,22–23)

- Post this question where all can see it: How can we become Easter people? Give each teen a pencil, a slip of white paper, and a plastic Easter egg—the colored kind that opens in half. Ask the young people to write their answer to the question on the slip of paper and put it inside the egg. Place the eggs in a large Easter basket. Have each person open an egg and share the answer with everyone. As a closing remark, note that as Easter people we are a sign of a new birth in Jesus through his Resurrection from the dead. (All readings)

- Have the teens make a large Easter greeting for the parish by creating giant letters that spell out the word *Alleluia!* Ask the teens to write their own Easter messages on the letters. Place the letters in a prominent place for all parishioners to see, with an invitation to the parishioners to add their own greetings and blessings. (Acts 10:34,37–43; Col. 3:1–4)

Second Sunday of Easter

Scripture Readings (45)

❖ Acts 4:32–35
❖ Ps. 118:2–4,13–15,22–24
❖ 1 John 5:1–6
❖ John 20:19–31

God's Word

A major theme of the Scripture readings is "Jesus in the flesh."

The reading from Acts reflects the powerful effect the Resurrection had on individual believers and on the Christian community. It describes a Christian community in which everyone shares what they have with others. Bearing witness is much more important than collecting wealth. They act with one heart and one mind, and the Spirit is at work in their ministry.

The psalm is a prayer of thanksgiving for God's mercy. The first verse emphasizes again and again that God's mercy endures forever. The psalmist finds courage in the Lord even when the psalmist feels he is falling. Again we hear, like last week, that the cornerstone that was once rejected is now the most essential of all.

The second reading shows us that faith and love are inseparable in the life of a Christian. Faith can overcome the evil in the world. The love of Christians for one another reflects the love of God. The water and blood mentioned here allude to the waters of baptism and the blood of the Crucifixion.

In last Sunday's Gospel reading, Jesus' followers found an empty tomb, with no sign of Jesus. In this Sunday's Gospel, Jesus comes to them later that night and stands before them, even though the doors are locked. The first words Jesus says are, "Peace be with you." As additional evidence that it is really he who suffered and died, he shows them the wounds in his hands and side. Then Jesus sends them forth to forgive the sins of others. He promises them the gift of the Holy Spirit so that they will be the "flesh" of Jesus to carry on his mission.

Thomas isn't there the first time Jesus appears, and he has trouble believing what he is told. A week later Jesus appears again with the same greeting, "Peace be with you." Jesus shows Thomas his wounds. At once, Thomas confesses his faith. Jesus blesses those who believe without seeing—Christians such as ourselves.

Themes for Teens

The following themes from the Scriptures relate to the lives of teens:
- Act with one heart and one mind.
- God will love us forever.
- If you love Jesus, you love God.
- Peace be with you.
- Do not doubt. See and believe.

Our Response

Activity

The Voice of Thomas

This activity is keyed to the Gospel reading. It offers a glimpse into what Thomas might have been thinking before and after Jesus appeared to him. It invites the teens to reflect on their own doubts and offer them to God.

Ask one young person to read today's Gospel passage. After a pause for silent reflection, ask another person to read "The Voice of Thomas."

"The Voice of Thomas"
I thought they were crazy—a bunch of men gone mad
    by grief, mad enough to believe in ghosts.
The doors were locked; no one could get into that room.

I told them to prove it to me, prove to me that they
    had seen Jesus walk again on the earth.
When I see the places the nails cut his flesh—
    then I will believe.

How I was to regret those words.
Soon, later, he stood before me—my Lord and my God—in the flesh,
offering to let me examine his hands, to put my hand in his side.

I deserved to be cast out for my doubt,
How could I have doubted my friend, my savior, my Lord?

Yet he did not send me away.
He said, "Peace be with you."
And never have I felt such peace.

My Lord and my God!

Allow the teens to spend some time writing in their journal about the times in their life when they have wondered about and even had doubts about their faith. Have them conclude their reflections with a prayer asking for God's help in overcoming these doubts.

Activity Ideas

The following activity ideas also relate to the Scripture readings. You may want to read the passage(s) indicated as part of the activity.

- Sight is a great gift. Jesus says faith is an even greater gift. Instruct the teens to list some of the gifts God has given them that they can actually see. Direct them to make another list of the gifts God has given them that are intangible. Challenge the teens to explain why they believe these gifts exist when they cannot see them. (John 20:19–31)

- Divide the teens into two teams—one that will present the case that Jesus exists, the other that will show that Jesus' tangible existence is not possible. One team will defend what we believe. The other will argue from the viewpoint that it is possible to know only with our sensory powers. After the debate, reflect on Jesus' statement: "'Blest are they who have not seen and have believed.'" (John 20:19–31)

- Read aloud the first part of today's Gospel and stop after Jesus' greeting of peace. Sing the song "Peace Prayer," by John Foley (*Glory and Praise,* vol. 1, no. 40), followed by offering one another a sign of Christ's peace. Then ask the young people, Why do you think this greeting is included in our celebration of the Eucharist? (John 20:19–31)

- After reading today's psalm, invite the teens to write thank-you notes to God for helping them get through the season of Lent and for the glorious gift of the Resurrection. (Ps. 118:2–4,13–15,22–24)

Third Sunday of Easter

Scripture Readings
(48)
- ❖ Acts 3:13–15,17–19
- ❖ Ps. 4:2,4,7–8,9
- ❖ 1 John 2:1–5
- ❖ Luke 24:35–48

God's Word

A major theme of the Scripture readings is "A message of peace."

In the reading from Acts, Peter, having healed a man who was lame, preaches the Christian message to the Jews in Jerusalem. He describes their part in the death of Jesus. But he also explains that they acted out of ignorance. In this light, God turns human failings into something good. They now have the opportunity to give witness to God's raising of Jesus from the dead, by repenting and changing their way of life.

Today's psalm asks God to look upon the people with love. Besides pleading for mercy, the psalmist also asks God to hear and answer his prayers when he is in trouble. The psalmist feels secure in God's love, so he is able to sleep better at night. God has taken care of us before, and we can be confident that God will always be there for us.

The First Letter of John tells us that the sure way of knowing God is to keep the Commandments that God gave us. In keeping the Commandments, the love of God is made perfect in us. John wants his friends to avoid sin, but tells them they should not fear if they fail because forgiveness is available through Jesus.

In Luke's account of Jesus appearing to the disciples after the Resurrection, the disciples still need to be convinced of his identity. Jesus calms their fears and assures them that they are not seeing a ghost. He eats a meal with them, shows them his hands and feet, and explains that the Messiah had to suffer to be raised up on the third day. They now see that the Risen Jesus present to them and the earthly Jesus they have known are one and the same person.

Jesus' greeting of peace each time he sees the disciples is both a greeting of peace and a gesture of forgiveness. The Easter message is peace.

Themes for Teens

The following themes from the Scriptures relate to the lives of teens:
- Change your ways; turn to God.
- Sleep in peace.
- Jesus takes away our sins.
- The Scriptures are fulfilled.
- Jesus' gift is peace.

Our Response

Activity   Peace Quilt

This craft project is keyed to the Gospel reading. It invites the teens to share Jesus' message of peace by creating a peace quilt. This material prayer helps us reflect on the need to work for peace at all levels of our relationships with others.

Provide the teens with a variety of colors and types of fabric, along with scissors and glue. Give each teen a 1-foot square piece of felt and permanent markers. Ask them to create a message of peace on their quilt square, using words and symbols. They can make up their own quotes or use quotes about peace from the Scriptures or famous people. They can focus on personal peace, peace in the family, peace in the neighborhood, or world peace.

Give the teens an opportunity to share the meaning of their quilt square with the group. Then stitch the squares together into one large quilt to hang in your meeting space, school lobby, or parish commons as a message and reminder of the need to work for peace in our family, community, and world.

Activity Ideas

The following activity ideas also relate to the Scripture readings. You may want to read the passage(s) indicated as part of the activity.

- Based on the readings from this week, give everyone a recipe card and ask them to write their own recipe for forgiveness. Invite them to share their ideas in a small-group discussion. (All readings)

- Give each teen a paper book cover. Tell them that it is the cover of the book of their life, and they have to think of a title for it. In small groups, have them share how they arrived at their title. Next, ask them to reflect on the question, If Jesus is the author of life, what would you want him to write in your book? Direct the teens to write their reflections on the inside of their book cover. (Acts 3:13–15,17–19)

- Send the teens on a language scavenger hunt. As preparation for a class or group meeting, ask them to learn how to say the word *peace* in as many languages as they can. After sharing the words with one another, write these words on a peace banner to hang in your meeting space. Teach everyone in the group to say "peace" in each language. (Luke 24:35–48)

- Lead a group discussion on the meaning of the following part of the Lord's Prayer: "Forgive us our sins as we forgive those who sin against us." (Acts 3:13–15,17–19; 1 John 2:1–5; Luke 24:35–48)

Fourth Sunday of Easter

Scripture Readings (51)

- ❖ Acts 4:8–12
- ❖ Ps. 118:1,8–9,21–23,26,21,29
- ❖ 1 John 3:1–2
- ❖ John 10:11–18

God's Word

A major theme of the Scripture readings is "The voice of the shepherd."

The reading from Acts shows the early Christian community continuing the work of Jesus and celebrating the power to heal and save in Jesus' name. Peter is in a lot of trouble with the Jewish leaders because he is preaching and healing in Jesus' name. The healing miracle is a sign of the salvation that came in Jesus, but Peter is still rejected by those who will not accept Jesus' messiahship. They do not believe that the only path to salvation is through Jesus.

Today's responsorial psalm repeats the theme of the last four Sundays: "The stone that the builders rejected has become the cornerstone." Rejected by Israel, Jesus is now the very foundation of faith. We are told to trust the Lord instead of earthly princes. This is a psalm of thanksgiving all the way through, and we are told that those who do all in the Lord's name will be blessed.

In First John, Christians are called children of God who enjoy a very close relationship with God. Unfortunately, being God's children is not without risk. The world fails to recognize them. At the same time, being children of God promises a remarkable future.

In today's reading from the Gospel of John, Jesus likens himself to a humble shepherd. But unlike shepherds who work for pay and might abandon the sheep when danger appears, Jesus lays down his life for his sheep. Jesus regards all people as his sheep, not just those who join his flock as Christians.

We, as Christian members of Jesus' flock, are called to be shepherds like him—not to lead with power and ambition, but to put the welfare of others before our own welfare.

Themes for Teens

The following themes from the Scriptures relate to the lives of teens:
- The name of Jesus saves.
- Jesus is our cornerstone.
- We are children of God.
- Listen to the voice of Jesus.
- Jesus is the Good Shepherd.

Our Response

Activity

The Voice of the Shepherd

This activity is keyed to the Gospel reading, in which the sheep recognize and listen to the voice of the shepherd. This discussion challenges the teens to reflect on how, as members of Jesus' flock, they recognize and listen to his voice in their life.

Read today's Gospel passage. Next, ask the young people to discuss the following questions, first in small groups and then as an entire group:
- How do we hear the voice of the Good Shepherd in our everyday life?
- What are some of the other voices that distract us from listening to the Lord's voice?
- Who are some of the people who help us hear the voice of Jesus?
- How can our voices become more like the voice of the Good Shepherd?

Activity Ideas

The following activity ideas also relate to the Scripture readings. You may want to read the passage(s) indicated as part of the activity.

- Share today's Gospel reading and then invite the teens to read and reflect on Psalm 23. Ask them how this psalm can be a source of comfort during rough times in their life. (John 10:11–18)

- Have the young people explore what their parish community is doing in the area of pastoral care. Invite someone involved in this work to share with the group some information about her or his ministry. Encourage the teens to suggest ways they can help reach out to people in their community who are homebound or hospitalized. (John 10:11–18)

Easter

- Invite the young people to share examples of times when they have felt left out or rejected. Ask them how it felt to be rejected. Then ask them whether their group has ever been unfriendly to a newcomer. Brainstorm ways the group can be more welcoming. (Ps. 118:1,8–9,21–23,26,21,29)

- Have the teens list the qualities of the Good Shepherd in their journal. Ask them to reflect on and write about which of these qualities they live by and which ones they need to work on in order to become more like the Good Shepherd. (John 10:11–18)

Fifth Sunday of Easter

Scripture Readings (54)

- ❖ Acts 9:26–31
- ❖ Ps. 22:26–27,28,30,31–32
- ❖ 1 John 3:18–24
- ❖ John 15:1–8

God's Word

A major theme of the Scripture readings is "Jesus is our vine."

In today's first reading, Saul (now Paul, after his conversion and baptism) tries to join the disciples of Jesus. Saul had previously made a habit of persecuting Christians, and the disciples are still afraid of him. However, Barnabas intercedes and says that Paul has seen and talked with the Lord and is now spreading the Gospel of Jesus. But speaking about Jesus is dangerous. There is an attempt on Paul's life. The disciples send him away for protection. The new church, despite its struggles, is growing and thriving.

Psalm 22 is a praise and promise psalm. The psalmist calls on families, nations, and all the earth to praise God. This psalm also reads as a public commitment to fulfill a promise of service and to pass on the message of salvation to future generations.

The second reading says that it is not enough just to talk about Jesus, faith must be expressed through action. We hear again God's great commandments—to have faith in Jesus and to love one another.

In the reading from John's Gospel, Jesus uses the image of the vine and branches to show how important it is to stay connected to him, to keep growing in faith. God is the vine grower. Jesus is the vine. We are the branches. The vine also represents the Christian community. The Christian community is fruitful if it proclaims and witnesses the Gospel to others. Those who hide their faith are like dead branches that need to be pruned.

Themes for Teens

The following themes from the Scriptures relate to the lives of teens:
- Jesus can change hearts.
- Pass on the faith.
- Praise God.
- Jesus is the vine; we are the branches.
- How do you bear fruit?

Our Response

Activity   Branching Out

These activities are keyed to all the readings. They encourage the teens to branch out beyond their own group to welcome and include others—Catholics and non-Catholics alike.

In Acts we read that we should welcome enemies as well as friends. Psalm 22 tells us to pass on our faith. The passage from First John says our faith is nothing without action, and the Gospel says we are like dead branches if we do not share our faith with others.

In response to the readings, urge the teens to do some of the following:

- Invite another group to join your group for a discussion or prayer service.
- Give a teacher of a younger CCD class a break by helping to teach the students.
- Put on a play or entertain senior citizens with contemporary renditions of Bible stories.
- Plan a social event and invite teens from other churches and denominations.
- Invite the pastor and parish staff to your meeting. After reading the Gospel, ask the teens to give the homily. Allow the pastor and staff to put their feet up and listen.

Activity Ideas

The following activity ideas also relate to the Scripture readings. You may want to read the passage(s) indicated as part of the activity.

- Note that the vine helps the branches stay alive by providing nourishment from the earth, water, and sun. Lead a discussion based on the following questions:
  - How does our faith get nourished?
  - How are our families, our friends, the church, the Scriptures, and the sacraments like vines that provide nourishment for our faith growth?
    (John 15:1–8)

- Place a bowl of fruit in the center of your group. Ask everyone to choose a piece of fruit as a symbol of their self and explain how it represents them.

  Next, ask the teens to describe how various pieces of fruit are symbols of good works they can do. For example, "I am like a banana because I like to tell jokes and make people laugh." Or "I would like to be like an apple you give to a teacher because I'd like to be more thoughtful of others." Allow them also to pick fruits that might not be in the bowl. (John 15:1–8)

- In their journal, have the teens answer these questions:
  - What branches must I prune from my life in order to bear more fruit?
  - What changes could I make that would allow me to grow and thrive?
    (John 15:1–8)

- Note that in the first reading the disciples were wary of Saul. They weren't sure who they should welcome to their community. Challenge the teens to examine how they treat new people in their school or neighborhood. Brainstorm concrete ways they could be more welcoming, both individually and as a community. (Acts 9:26–31)

Sixth Sunday of Easter

Scripture Readings (57)

❖ Acts 10:25–26,34–35,44–48
❖ Ps. 98:1–4
❖ 1 John 4:7–10
❖ John 15:9–17

God's Word

A major theme of the Scripture readings is "God is love."

The young church was grappling with questions of membership. Who should belong? Who should be baptized? In the reading from Acts, Peter says that God shows no partiality. As a sign of God's impartiality, the Spirit comes upon all the listeners—Gentiles as well as Jews. All who believe are baptized in the name of Jesus and welcomed into the new church.

The responsorial psalm announces that God's salvation is not just for Israel, but for other people as well.

The second reading and the Gospel are love letters from God. For the writer of First John, the message is simple: God loves us and is the source of our love for one another. This love is revealed through the gift of Jesus Christ and his offering of his life for our sins.

In the reading from John's Gospel, we learn that to love means to participate in the love between God the Father and Jesus. Jesus' commandment is to "'love one another as I have loved you.'" In last week's readings, our relationship with Jesus was described as branches on the vine. This week we are invited to be part of Jesus' inner circle—one of his closest friends. We are called again to bear fruit by loving one another.

Themes for Teens

The following themes from the Scriptures relate to the lives of teens:
• God is love.
• Love one another.
• God's love doesn't discriminate.
• Jesus calls us friends.
• Jesus has chosen us.

Our Response

Activity

Christian Love Versus Worldly Love

This discussion activity is keyed to the second reading and the Gospel reading. It asks the young people to compare and contrast the image of love portrayed in today's readings with society's view of love.
• Ask the teens to read today's Scripture passages and list the attributes of love found in them.
• Show some video clips recorded earlier from MTV. Direct the teens to list the qualities of love as depicted on MTV.
• Select several magazine ads in which some sort of image of love is used to hawk products. Instruct the teens to list the qualities of love found in these advertisements.
• Play a few snippets from songs that glamorize exploitative love. Have the teens list the images of love found in these lyrics.

- Show a scene from a daytime soap opera, preferably one in which love is used as a form of manipulation. Ask the teens how love is used as a weapon.
- Close by emphasizing how radical the selfless love of Jesus is in today's society, but also how it is an ideal goal to work toward.

Activity Ideas

The following activity ideas also relate to the Scripture readings. You may want to read the passage(s) indicated as part of the activity.

- Hold a Valentine's Day in May. Invite the teens to study the Scriptures and learn more about what they teach about love. Have them make Valentine's cards with Scripture passages on love as the centerpiece. Encourage them to send their cards to loved ones as a reminder of God's love in their life. (John 15:9–17)

- Before the group meeting, ask each teen to buy or make a greeting card for God. Form small groups and ask the teens to share why they selected or designed the card they did and how it describes their relationship with God. (Ps. 98:1–4)

- Invite the teens to bring CDs or cassettes of love songs to class. Play a snippet of a song and ask them how they can apply the words to their relationship with Jesus. Use as many of the teens' songs as you can. (1 John 4:7–10; John 15:9–17)

- In small groups, have the teens debate this question: Is love a decision or a feeling? Direct them to use examples to make their point. Have them share their arguments with the large group. (1 John 4:7–10; John 15:9–17)

Seventh Sunday of Easter

Scripture Readings (61)

- ❖ Acts 1:15–17,20–26
- ❖ Ps. 103:1–2,11–12,19–20
- ❖ 1 John 4:11–16
- ❖ John 17:11–19

God's Word

A major theme of the Scripture readings is "Discipleship."

The first reading describes the naming of someone to take the place of Judas as one of the Twelve Apostles. The qualifications to become an Apostle are that one had to have walked with Jesus from the time of his baptism by John and to have been a witness to the Resurrection. They make nominations and cast lots among them. Matthias is chosen. The other Apostles were chosen by Jesus at the beginning of his ministry. Matthias is chosen by inviting the Risen Lord into the process to help the Apostles discern.

Today's blessing psalm portrays God as a benevolent king of a mighty kingdom—worthy of blessings received for kindness and forgiveness.

The reading from First John continues the second reading from last week and reinforces the message of God's great love for us. No one has ever seen God, but when Christians love one another, God is revealed in that love. When we love one another, God dwells within us.

In the reading from John's Gospel, Jesus asks God the Father to bless and protect the disciples. In this intimate conversation with God, Jesus talks about his return to his Father. Jesus did his best to protect and guide his followers and now, as he is about to die, he turns them over to God's care.

Jesus does not pray for the Apostles to be removed from the world and its dangers. Rather, he prays that they will always have truth—that is, the fulfillment of his words—on their side as he sends them into the world to proclaim the Good News. Jesus prays not only for his immediate disciples but also for all those after them who will preach and teach the Good News.

Themes for Teens

The following themes from the Scriptures relate to the lives of teens:
- Pray when you have a decision to make.
- God is love.
- God dwells in us.
- God watches over us.
- The Gospel is our mission.

Our Response

Activity

I See God in You

This affirmation activity is keyed to the second reading. It helps the teens recognize God in one another.

Mention that the reading tells us that no one has ever seen God, but if we love one another, God dwells in us. In the Gospel, we learn that we are protected by God's name.

Then give the teens each a small piece of white poster board. Ask them to write their name vertically across the top of the poster board. Direct them to use their name as an acrostic, by attaching to it names for God that begin with a letter of their name. For example, they can use the name Lord if their name has an *l* in it. When they are finished, tell them to attach their poster to a wall of your meeting space.

Next, direct the teens to move from poster to poster, using markers to add affirming words and phrases that describe ways they recognize God in each person, again using a letter in the person's name as the first letter in their affirming word(s). Stress that all notations are to be positive. Encourage the teens to take their poster home after the activity.

Activity Ideas

The following activity ideas also relate to the Scripture readings. You may want to read the passage(s) indicated as part of the activity.

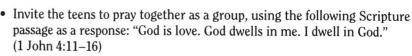

- Invite the teens to pray together as a group, using the following Scripture passage as a response: "God is love. God dwells in me. I dwell in God." (1 John 4:11–16)

- Note that in the Gospel, Jesus offers a special prayer for his friends. Then give everyone a piece of notepaper and an envelope. Invite them to write a special prayer asking God to help one of their friends. Encourage them to send or give the prayer to this friend. (John 17:11–19)

- Read today's Gospel passage together. Then join in praying the Lord's Prayer. Ask the teens to explain what the prayer of Jesus in the Gospel has in common with the Lord's Prayer? (John 17:11–19)

- Direct the teens to call out some of the strategies they use for making decisions. If prayer is not mentioned by anyone, read today's first reading aloud and talk about the importance of including God in our decision making. Encourage the teens to reflect on a decision they are in the process of making and to invite God to help guide them. (Acts 1:15–17,20–26)

Pentecost Sunday

Scripture Readings (64)
- ❖ Acts 2:1–11
- ❖ Ps. 104:1,24,29–30,31,34
- ❖ 1 Cor. 12:3–7,12–13
- ❖ John 20:19–23

God's Word

A major theme of the Scripture readings is "One in the Holy Spirit."

All of today's readings speak about the Spirit of Jesus gifting his disciples with the talents and powers for going forth with courage to proclaim the Good News.

The first reading, from Acts, describes the events of Pentecost, in which the Holy Spirit comes upon the Apostles in wind and fire. When they are filled with the Holy Spirit, they begin to speak in languages they never knew before. The crowd assembled is astonished. Though many of the crowd are foreigners, they understand that the disciples are speaking about the wonders of God. God has reversed the Tower of Babel. Rather than being confused by the different languages, the people can understand them.

Psalm 104 is a hymn of praise to God, who sends forth the Spirit to renew the face of the whole earth.

The second reading is a reminder that the Spirit bestows gifts for proclaiming the Good News on everyone, but not everyone has the same kinds of gifts. The gifts of the Spirit are public gifts, not private ones. And when people use them to complement the gifts of others, the community forms the one Body of Christ in which the Spirit is alive.

The early Christians probably argued about whose gifts were the most important. As one Body in Christ, divisions such as race, age, or nationality lose all meaning. The image of the body was chosen to highlight that the community is not a static, unmoving group. A living body grows and moves and changes, so, too, does the church community if it is to stay alive.

Today's reading from the Gospel of John is Jesus' promise of the Holy Spirit. The disciples are hiding out, scared and defeated. Jesus comes to them and breathes new life into them—the breath of the Spirit. With the gift of the Spirit comes the gift of peace and a mandate to go out and forgive the sins of others.

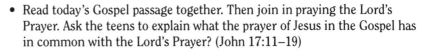

Easter

Themes for Teens The following themes from the Scriptures relate to the lives of teens:
- Be filled with the Holy Spirit.
- Lord, send us your Spirit.
- Our gifts are to serve.
- We are the Body of Christ.
- The Spirit offers us peace.

Our Response

Activity One in the Spirit

This activity is keyed to all the readings. It helps the teens focus on the evil of discrimination and on how, in the Spirit of God, the human race is united.

Ask the teens to give examples of some of the forces that divide our community, such as race, gender, economic inequality, and age.

Direct each small group of teens to pick one of these divisive issues and do the following:

1. Give current examples of this divisive issue from the news or other media.
2. List some strategies for fighting this form of discrimination.

Close by discussing ways they can celebrate diversity. Challenge the teens to take the first steps against discrimination in their own community.

Activity Ideas The following activity ideas also relate to the Scripture readings. You may want to read the passage(s) indicated as part of the activity.

- Ask the teens to take a few minutes to be still and listen to their breathing. Note that breath is essential to who we are, yet we rarely notice it or think about it. Invite them to reflect on how the breath of the Holy Spirit is essential to our faith. (Acts 2:1–11; John 20:19–23)

- Learn a prayer or a hymn in another language. Share your prayer or hymn with the group and celebrate the diversity of the Catholic community. (1 Cor. 12:3–7,12–13)

- Give the teens a list of summer ministries and encourage them to use the gifts the Spirit has bestowed on them to get involved in the life of the church over the summer months. (All readings)

- Challenge the teens to name all seven gifts of the Holy Spirit: wisdom, understanding, knowledge, courage, right judgment, reverence, and wonder and awe. Ask them what other gifts they think come from the Holy Spirit? Add these to the list. Inquire as to how they can serve others with these gifts. (All readings)

Trinity Sunday

Scripture Readings (166)

- ❖ Deut. 4:32–34,39–40
- ❖ Ps. 33:4–5,6,9,18–19,20,22
- ❖ Rom. 8:14–17
- ❖ Matt. 28:16–20

God's Word

A major theme of the Scripture readings is "One God in three."

In the first reading, Moses puts a series of questions to the people. He is trying to help them recognize the power and glory of God as well as the favor of God that now rests on them. The people now see in their hearts that there is no other than the Lord, their God. If they are faithful to God's commandments, they will have a long life.

The psalm praises the fidelity of God and calls for confidence in the God whose works are seen in creation. God protects and takes care of those who place their hope in God.

The reading from Romans names Christians as children of God. In Jesus Christ, Christians are no longer slaves, but are part of God's family. We can call God *Abba,* which is similar to our word *Daddy.* As children of God in Jesus, we must suffer with him. But as God's heirs in Jesus, we will also participate in his glorification.

In the reading from Matthew's Gospel, Jesus commissions the disciples to go forth and make disciples of all nations of people—to baptize them into the family of God in the name of the Father, the Son, and the Holy Spirit.

Themes for Teens

The following themes from the Scriptures relate to the lives of teens:
- Fix God in your heart.
- God had chosen us.
- We are children of God.
- God is a family.
- Share the Gospel with all.

Our Response

Activity

Baptized to Follow the Cross

This activity is keyed to the Gospel reading. As your academic year draws to an end for the summer months, you can commission the young people as Jesus commissioned the disciples in today's Gospel reading.

Proclaim today's Gospel reading and allow the teens a few minutes to discuss in pairs the message they hear. Lead them in the renewal of their baptismal promises, which serves as a reminder of their baptismal call to serve. Bless water. Then invite the teens one at a time to dip their hand in the water and make the sign of the cross to signify their acceptance of the commission to proclaim God to others.

Easter

Activity Ideas
The following activity ideas also relate to the Scripture readings. You may want to read the passage(s) indicated as part of the activity.

- Pray the Glory Be, a traditional Catholic prayer, with your group.

  Glory be to the Father,
  and to the Son,
  and to the Holy Spirit.
  As it was in the beginning,
  is now, and ever shall be,
  world without end.
  Amen.

  (All readings)

- Mention that at the end of today's Gospel reading, Jesus promises, "'I am with you always.'" In their journal, have the teens write down some of the ways they feel Jesus' presence in their everyday life. (Matt. 28:16–20)

- Ask the teens what they mean when they bless themselves and say, "In the name of the Father, and of the Son, and of the Holy Spirit. Amen." Urge them to reflect on the way they reach out to the community as individuals and as a group. Invite them to answer the following questions:
  - What do you do in the name of the Father?
  - What do you do in the name of the Son?
  - What do you do in the name of the Spirit?

  (All readings)

- Ask the teens to begin their prayer each day this week by calling on God as "Daddy." Ask them later how they felt about talking to God in this way. How is it different from the other relationships we have with God as creator, king, judge, and the like? (Rom. 8:14–17)

Corpus Christi Sunday

**Scripture Readings
(169)**
❖ Exod. 24:3–8
❖ Ps. 116:12–13,15–16,17–18
❖ Heb. 9:11–15
❖ Mark 14:12–16,22–26

God's Word
A major theme of the Scripture readings is "The body and blood of Christ."

The reading from the Book of Exodus describes the ritual that sealed the Covenant God made with Moses and the people at Mount Sinai. After listening to an account of God's side of the Covenant, the people vow to do everything God tells them to do. The sprinkling of blood on the people is a symbol of the unification of God and the people.

The writer of the psalm offers up the cup of salvation as a ritual sealing of God's Covenant with the people and as a way of thanking God for all that has been given.

The reading from Hebrews tells us about Jesus, the great high priest, who offered the perfect sacrifice to God. Jesus did not offer sacrifices of animals, but spilled his own blood so that we might be freed from sin.

The reading from Mark's Gospel is an account of the Last Supper, in which Jesus breaks bread that he identifies with his body and shares a cup of wine that he identifies with his blood. This meal with its ritual of sacrifice and thanksgiving has become our Eucharist and is the center of our faith as Catholic Christians.

Corpus Christi is the celebration of the body and blood of Christ given to us as the sign and seal of God's Covenant with us.

Themes for Teens   The following themes from the Scriptures relate to the lives of teens:
- Jesus is the new covenant.
- Drink the cup of salvation.
- We will do what God asks.
- "This is my body; this is my blood."

Our Response

Activity   **You Are What You Eat**

This activity is keyed to the Gospel reading. Direct the teens to write the following expression in their journal: "You are what you eat." Then tell them to apply this statement to the Mass, explaining what it might tell us about receiving Jesus regularly in the Eucharist.

Here are some questions based on today's readings, which the teens could respond to in their journal:
- How is Jesus' sacrifice a perfect sacrifice?
- What does it mean to drink the cup of salvation?
- What is most difficult to understand about the mystery of bread and wine changing into Christ's body and blood during the Eucharist?
- How can we avoid taking the gift of the Eucharist for granted?

Activity Ideas   The following activity ideas also relate to the Scripture readings. You may want to read the passage(s) indicated as part of the activity.

- Instruct the teens to compare and contrast a traditional North American Thanksgiving dinner with the Christian celebration of the Eucharist. (Mark 14:12–16,22–26)

- Read the passage from Exodus to the group and note that in the reading the people say yes to God's Covenant. Then ask the teens to find—in both the Hebrew and Christian Scriptures—examples of other people who said yes to God. (Exod. 24:3–8)

- Explain that in Moses' time, the blood of animals was used in rituals to seal promises and symbolize union with God, but Jesus shed his own blood to seal and unite us with God. Then pose these questions:
  - What are some of the rituals we use to seal promises and symbolize unions with others?
  - What are some of the ways we seal promises and symbolize union with God?

(All readings)

- Arrange to celebrate a traditional Jewish Seder meal, similar to the one Jesus shared with his friends at the Last Supper. After doing so, discuss how the liturgy of the Eucharist mirrors this ancient tradition. (Mark 14:12–16,22–26)

Ordinary Time

Second Sunday of the Year

Scripture Readings (66)

- ❖ 1 Sam. 3:3–10,19
- ❖ Ps. 40:2,4,7–8,10
- ❖ 1 Cor. 6:13–15,17–20
- ❖ John 1:35–42

God's Word

A major theme of the Scripture readings is "God's call and our response."

The story of Samuel's call in the first reading indicates that the call of the Lord can be confused with the call of other people and the attraction of things. Help may be needed to recognize God's voice. When one recognizes God's voice, it takes courage to reply, "Speak Lord, for your servant is listening," and to say as the psalmist, "Here I am, Lord; I come to do your will."

Paul focuses God's call on challenges that continue in our world today. One challenge is to respect our body and the bodies of others when tempted by drugs, alcohol, premarital sex, and even junk food. Paul holds up the body as a gift from God to be treated as such. We are members of Christ's Body; we must respect others as part of that Body.

Like the first reading and the psalm, John's Gospel features God's call and our response. Jesus invites us to ponder the question, "'What are you looking for?'" We need to be open to the Lord working in our life, to recognize that he is calling us and to be ready to respond to the call.

Themes for Teens

The following themes from the Scriptures relate to the lives of teens:
- Here I am, Lord.
- Respect others.
- God is calling me, am I listening?
- What is God's will for me?
- If I come and see, what will I find?

Our Response

Activity

Body Language

This activity is keyed to the reading from First Corinthians. It invites the teens to explore these questions:
- If your body is a temple of the Holy Spirit, how do you treat it?
- If others are part of Christ's Body, how do you treat them?

Begin by displaying two posters of body outlines on the wall—one standing straight up, and another lying in a prone position. Have a number of colored markers available.

Direct the teens to describe some of the ways we fail to take good care of our body. As they respond, have them write their answer on the poster with the prone figure on it. Some examples are eating junk food, not getting enough sleep, biting our nails, overeating, and starving ourselves to appear thin.

Next, encourage them to think of some of the things we can do to take better care of our body. As they respond, tell them to write their answers on the poster with the upright figure on it. Some examples are getting plenty of exercise, avoiding alcohol and other drugs, eating healthy snacks, and quitting smoking or not starting.

Stress the need to view our body as a gift from God and that respect for others begins with a healthy respect and care for ourself.

Next, split the group by gender, sending the young men and young women to separate locations. Ask each group to answer the following questions:

- What bugs you most about the way members of the other sex treat you?
- What words or language do they use that sometimes makes you feel uncomfortable?
- What messages—positive and negative—can our body give without using words?
- How is respect for the body also respect for the person?

When the two groups come together, choose spokespersons to share responses to the questions. You can count on a lively exchange, but stress that all opinions are to be honored.

Activity Ideas

The following activity ideas also relate to the Scripture readings. You may want to read the passage(s) indicated as part of the activity.

- Invite parish ministers—ordained, religious, and lay—to give witness talks about the way they have answered God's call in their life. Hold an open forum afterward in which the teens can ask frank questions about the pros and cons of choosing one of these paths. (1 Sam. 3:3–10,19; John 1:35–42)

- Hold a discussion around the following question: Why are we sometimes afraid to say, "Here I am, Lord, I come to do your will"? Challenge each teen to think of ways that he or she does God's will or can do God's will at home, at school, with friends, in the parish community, and so forth. (1 Sam. 3:3–10,19)

- Ask the teens to spend some journal-writing time reflecting quietly on the question Jesus asks: "'What are you looking for?'" Invite them to write out ways that they are open to God working in their life. (John 1:35–42)

- Play the song "Come and See," by David Kauffman (from the recording *Come and See,* Music for Life, 1988). Lead a discussion, using the following questions:
  - When Jesus asked the disciples to follow him, what do you think they expected?
  - What did they have to give up to follow Jesus?
  - Was it always easy for them to follow Jesus?

(John 1:35–42)

Third Sunday of the Year

**Scripture Readings
(69)**

❖ Jon. 3:1–5,10
❖ Ps. 25:4–5,6–7,8–9
❖ 1 Cor. 7:29–31
❖ Mark 1:14–20

God's Word

A major theme of the Scripture readings is "The call to discipleship."

The passage from the Book of Jonah gives a perspective on the mercy of God. It shows that God will forgive anyone who takes the call to conversion seriously. The Ninevites change their behavior and ways of living that led to evil and show by their actions that they are willing to embrace a new way of life. And God, to the dismay of Jonah, does not destroy them.

The psalm recognizes God as teacher and implores us to call upon the Lord to teach us the ways of the Lord. God is good and merciful. We are all welcome to walk in God's ways—even those who have taken the wrong path before—proud people and sinners.

Paul's letter is a wake-up call for all those who may become too worried about life in this world. The world as we know it is not the Kingdom God promised. We need to live in this world with one eye on the next. Paul has a sense of urgency about this because, at the time of this letter, he believed the Second Coming of Christ would occur in his lifetime.

Mark tells us how Jesus began his mission and called the first disciples. Jesus calls on all who will listen, saying, "'Reform your lives and believe in the good news.'" Jesus finds his first disciples in ordinary places doing ordinary things. He asks them to give up all they know and follow him. They are to become members of the Kingdom of God and to play an active role in establishing the Kingdom—to proclaim the Good News and be the Good News.

Themes for Teens

The following themes from the Scriptures relate to the lives of teens:
• Become a new you.
• Teach us your ways.
• Walk in Jesus' ways.
• Being a Christian is radical.
• Come, follow Jesus.

Our Response

Activity   Cast Out Your Nets

This prayer service is keyed to the Gospel reading. It uses the symbol of a fishing net as the focus for shared prayer and invites the young people to call on Jesus to help them live as his disciples.

Borrow a large fishing net (a net for protecting fruit and vegetables from birds will do) and spread it on the floor in your prayer space. Arrange chairs in a circle around it. Ask a teen to prepare and read the Gospel passage during the prayer. Invite an older teen or young adult to share the story of her or his personal call to ministry—how Jesus called her or him to reach out to others.

Ordinary Time

Use the following order, or a similar one, for the prayer service:

- *Call to prayer.*

- *Opening song.* "Come to the Water," by John Foley, vv. 1 and 2 (*Glory and Praise*, vol. 2, no. 92)

- *Reading.* Mark 1:14–20

- *Pause for quiet reflection.*

- *Witness talk.*

- *Shared prayer.* Introduce this prayer in the following way:
  Jesus calls us to be fishers of men and women. But it takes a lot of courage to cast out our net and reach out to God's people. Let us pray now to have the courage to share the Gospel message with others through our words and actions. In the center of our gathering is a net used by fishers. When you are ready to offer a prayer, pick up an end of the net and hold it in your hands. Keep holding onto your place in the net as the prayer continues.

- *Blessing.*
  Dear God, please bless your disciples gathered here.
  As this net connects us, draw us together in a common mission
  to live and share your Gospel. Amen.

- *Closing song.* "Come to the Water," by John Foley, vv. 3 and 4

Activity Ideas

The following activity ideas also relate to the Scripture readings. You may want to read the passage(s) indicated as part of the activity.

- Talk about the role of penance in reconciliation in the following terms: What is penance? How do we do it? Why do we do it? Why do we need to say we are sorry with our actions? Isn't just saying we are sorry enough? Share a story of forgiveness, a time when "actions spoke louder than words." (Jon. 3:1–5,10)

- Read the poem "The Road Not Taken," by Robert Frost. Challenge the teens to connect the poem with this week's psalm response. Ask them how following Jesus is following the road less traveled. How does following Jesus make a difference? (Ps. 25:4–5,6–7,8–9)

- Rent the video *O God!* starring George Burns and John Denver. After watching the film, ask the teens to share how they might react if they were in John Denver's shoes and Jesus came right up to them today and said, "Come follow me." (Mark 1:14–20)

- Send the teens out with a few cameras to capture ways parishioners witness for Jesus. Set up a bulletin board display with photos and captions to honor these folks and inspire others to join active parish ministry. (All readings)

- Instruct the teens to search the Christian Scriptures for passages in which Jesus talks about the Kingdom of Heaven. Contrast these descriptions with society's lure of "having it all," as portrayed in advertisements, movies, and so on. (Mark 1:14–20)

Fourth Sunday of the Year

Scripture Readings (72)

- ❖ Deut. 18:15–20
- ❖ Ps. 95:1–2,6–7,7–9
- ❖ 1 Cor. 7:32–35
- ❖ Mark 1:21–28

God's Word

A major theme of the Scripture readings is "Listen to the prophets."

The passage from Deuteronomy is the basis of the Jewish belief that the Messiah, a savior, would be a prophet like Moses. Christians see this belief fulfilled in Jesus.

The psalm calls us to greet the voice of the Lord and to listen with an open heart.

Paul serves as a pastor to the Christian community at Corinth. He calls them to look at their lives and at those things that get in the way of their relationship with Jesus. In effect, Paul is a prophet to that community and likewise serves as a prophet to us. The reading challenges us to promote good in our community and to promote that which will help us devote ourselves to the Lord.

In the passage from Mark's Gospel, Jesus expels a demon from a man. Jesus shows he has the authority to speak and act as a prophet sent by God. His exorcism of the demon demonstrates that good triumphs over evil. This miracle is the first of many Mark records to show both the authority and the compassion of Jesus. This passage also reveals the main work of Jesus—the work of forgiving, healing, and teaching in the name of God.

Themes for Teens

The following themes from the Scriptures relate to the lives of teens:

- God speaks through prophets.
- Open your heart to God.
- Find room for the Lord.
- Make time for God.
- Good wins over evil.

Our Response

Activity

Profiting from Prophets

This activity is keyed to all the readings. It is a research project that invites the teens to discern the differences between prophets of today who live and share the Gospel and false prophets who may lead them away from the Gospel.

Divide your group into three smaller groups. Give each small group one of the following three assignments:

1. Do some research on one of the prophets from the Hebrew Scriptures. Be prepared to proclaim some of the messages he or she shared. Prepare and perform a short skit on one scene from his or her life.

2. Identify some prophets of today—people who have made radical choices to live and proclaim the Gospel. Share some of their messages and perform a short skit about how they live their lives. Demonstrate how people respond to them.

3. Identify some false prophets of today. Look for those who lure others with promises of success, power, wealth, and fame. What are their empty messages? Show what they are really selling. Act out an "infomercial," trying to lead others the wrong way.

When the groups finish, call on a spokesperson from each group to share with the large group what her or his group discovered.

Note: If you are doing this activity in a class setting, it could be assigned as homework. If you are doing it in a youth group setting, you will need to provide each group with materials to get them started.

Activity Ideas The following activity ideas also relate to the Scripture readings. You may want to read the passage(s) indicated as part of the activity.

 • Read together today's psalm and its response. Have the teens discuss how Jesus takes our hearts of stone and turns them into hearts of flesh? What kinds of things harden our heart against God? (Ps. 95:1–2,6–7,7–9)

 • Invite the young people to keep track of how they spend their time each day. Have them draw the face of a clock with the hours numbered. Then instruct them to use one color to shade the hours that promote God in their life, as Paul requires, and another color to shade the hours that distract them and pull them away from God. (1 Cor. 7:32–35)

 • Give each small group a 3-minute hourglass egg timer. Pass the egg timer around to each person in the group. As each person receives the egg timer, he or she should describe some ways he or she can make more time to listen for God's voice. Give each person a chance to share. (1 Cor. 7:32–35)

 • Lead a discussion about Moses and Jesus as prophets, using the following discussion questions:
   ○ What are some characteristics that Moses and Jesus have in common?
   ○ What is it about Moses and Jesus that makes their teaching so compelling?
   ○ What makes a teacher or preacher attractive and convincing in our world?

(Mark 1:21–28)

Fifth Sunday of the Year

Scripture Readings (75)
- ❖ Job 7:1–4,6–7
- ❖ Ps. 147:1–2,3–4,5–6
- ❖ 1 Cor. 9:1–19,22–23
- ❖ Mark 1:29–39

God's Word

A major theme of the Scripture readings is "Hope in the Gospel of Jesus."

The reading from Job speaks of the burdens of the world and of the temptation to despair in the midst of them. In contrast, the psalmist offers hope that the Lord will be there to heal human brokenness.

Paul tells the Corinthians that as a Christian he has no choice but to preach the Gospel, and that in doing so, he will be blessed. The Good News of Jesus is not to be heard and stored away on a shelf, but rather lived and preached by us.

The Gospel of Mark offers hope in the face of human afflictions, as Jesus heals sick people and expels demons. Proclaiming the Gospel in word and action exhausts the body and spirit, so Jesus retreats to spend time in prayer. In doing so, he finds new vigor and strength to continue his mission of proclaiming the Good News.

Themes for Teens

The following themes from the Scriptures relate to the lives of teens:
- Bad things can happen to good people.
- God can fix broken hearts.
- It is everyone's job to share the Gospel.
- Jesus can cure what ails you.
- You've got to pray just to make it today.

Our Response

Activity

A Reply to Paul

This activity is keyed to the reading from First Corinthians. It invites the young people to recognize that Paul is writing to them personally and not only to the Corinthians. Ask the teens to spread out and be silent during this activity.

Give each teen a sheet of paper, a pencil, and a copy of the second reading. Tell them that they have just received this letter from their friend Paul, and they are to take a few minutes to read it and then compose a reply. The following prompts will help them get started:
- In what ways have you shared the Gospel?
- Have you ever turned away from the message of Jesus? In what ways?
- Describe an instance of being humble while preaching God's word?
- Who proclaimed the Gospel to you? How have you responded to it?
- What blessings have come when you have shared the Gospel?

A variation of this activity might include writing a response to Paul's letter from the entire community. How does your youth community live up to the challenge of sharing the Gospel?

Activity Ideas   The following activity ideas also relate to the Scripture readings. You may want to read the passage(s) indicated as part of the activity.

- Facilitate a large-group discussion on the challenges and obstacles of sharing the Gospel in our everyday life versus the rewards and blessings of doing so. (All readings)

- Send the teens to the Christian Scriptures to find other examples of Jesus healing the sick. Provide questions for small-group discussion on the importance of being healed in body and spirit. (Mark 1:29–39)

- Write the letters *H, O, P,* and *E,* each on a different piece of poster board. Also write on each poster the description found below of what that letter stands for. Challenge the teens to think of people they can lean on in times of despair, discouragement, and hopelessness. Invite them to list the names of these people on the appropriate poster.
  H = those we can go to *help* us when we are in trouble.
  O = those who are *open* to us when we need to talk.
  P = those we can *pray* with and share our faith.
  E = those who *encourage* us and support us to keep going.
                                                  (Ps. 147:1–2,3–4,5–6)

Sixth Sunday of the Year

Scripture Readings (78)
- ❖ Lev. 13:1–2,44–46
- ❖ Ps. 32:1–2,5,11
- ❖ 1 Cor. 10:31—11:1
- ❖ Mark 1:40–45

God's Word   A major theme of the Scripture readings is "Turn to the Lord to be healed."

The first reading relates an old Jewish practice of branding as unclean those who have leprosy and setting them apart from the community. It may also symbolize current practices of labeling persons and groups and excluding them from the community. The psalmist then tells us that we can attain acceptance and healing if we turn to the Lord.

In the reading from the First Letter to the Corinthians, Paul calls upon the people to build up the community by imitating him, who imitates Christ.

The leper in the Gospel reading did not wait for Jesus to come to him; he recognized his affliction and turned to Jesus for healing. Jesus healed him and sent him back to the community.

Themes for Teens   The following themes from the Scriptures relate to the lives of teens:
- We all need forgiveness.
- Turn to the Lord.
- Imitate Christ.
- Don't be afraid to ask God for help.
- God will heal our body and spirit.

Our Response

Turn Around

This prayer-writing activity is keyed to the psalm. It invites the teens to become psalmists themselves by rewriting the verses of a psalm in their own language.

Ask the teens to brainstorm a list of some "times of trouble" they might find themselves in. Suggest that they reflect on situations with family, friends, classmates, and the like. Then, working in small groups, have them rewrite the verses of the responsorial psalm in their own language, reflecting their experience of the need to be healed.

The finished psalms could be used for opening or closing prayers at a meeting or as part of a larger prayer service.

If the finished psalms are used as part of a larger prayer service, consider placing a large crucifix in the prayer space as the focal point. Invite the teens to turn toward the crucifix as part of their response when reading the psalm response, "I turn to you, Lord, in times of trouble, and you fill me with the joy of salvation."

Activity Ideas

The following activity ideas also relate to the Scripture readings. You may want to read the passage(s) indicated as part of the activity.

- Start with a game of Follow the Leader. Lead into a discussion on the difference between imitating Christ and following him blindly. Challenge the teens to make decisions by following Jesus' example, even when doing so means not following the crowd. (1 Cor. 10:31—11:1)

- Invite the teens each to make a small mask from a brown paper grocery bag. On the inside of their mask, direct them to write some things they have done that they are not proud of. On the outside, have them write things they do to hide these failures. The masks can be destroyed as part of an unmasking ritual for finding and claiming their true self. (Lev. 13:1–2,44–46)

- Send the teens to the Scriptures to find examples of the way Jesus treated others. Initiate a small-group discussion on some of the ways we can imitate Christ in our everyday life. (1 Cor. 10:31—11:1)

- During shared prayer, offer the names of family and friends who are in need of healing right now. Stress the importance of the youth community in supporting these people with prayer. (Mark 1:40–45)

Ordinary Time

Seventh Sunday of the Year

Scripture Readings (81)

- ❖ Isa. 43:18–19,21–22,24–25
- ❖ Ps. 41:2–3,4–5,13–14
- ❖ 2 Cor. 1:18–22
- ❖ Mark 2:1–12

God's Word

A major theme of the Scripture readings is "The need for forgiveness and healing."

In Isaiah, the prophet says that God is not a God who holds grudges. God is a God of second chances, the one who makes all things—including us—new again.

The psalmist comes to God asking for forgiveness, recognizing that people need healing. God is approachable, not some distant, uncaring being, and we can go to God when misfortune or sickness befalls us.

Paul tells the Corinthians that God's promise is fulfilled through the Son, Jesus Christ. God never tells us no when called upon; God answers yes when needed. God is not fickle—there for us one minute and abandoning us the next. As in the first reading and the psalm, this reading assures us that God is always present with us.

The Gospel passage begins with an act of faith by four men who bring a friend to Jesus to be cured. Jesus cures the man and forgives his sins. This shows that Jesus' power to heal comes from his relationship with God. We know we can go to Jesus when we need healing of both our physical and spiritual selves.

Themes for Teens

The following themes from the Scriptures relate to the lives of teens:
- God makes everything new.
- God does not hold a grudge.
- Bring friends to Jesus for healing.
- Jesus is God's yes to us.
- Our God is a merciful God.
- Jesus heals our body and soul.

Our Response

Activity   Say Yes to God

This activity is keyed to the first two readings and the psalm. It invites the teens to look at ways we turn away from God in sin, and the amazing mercy of Jesus found in the Scriptures. It invites them to say yes to God.

Read the first reading, the psalm, and the second reading from today's Scriptures before beginning this activity, or space the readings in between parts of the activity.

On the far left side of a chalkboard (or sheet of newsprint), draw a large half circle, open to the right, with the word *God* in it. On the far right side, draw another large half circle, open to the left, with the word *Me* in it. Write the word *No* in the middle of the board. Ask the teens to think about and share some of the ways we sin and turn away from God. As they name each sin, ask them to come up and write it on the chalkboard under the word *No.* Some examples are gossiping, disobeying, cursing, and lying. As each example is written, have the writer also close a small part of the open half circle with *Me* in it. Continue with examples and the closing of the circle until the word *Me* is entirely enclosed.

Next, ask the teens to find a partner. Give each pair a Bible. Direct them to come up with two examples of God's mercy—one from the Scriptures and one from the world around them.

Replace the word *No* on the blackboard with the word *Yes,* written in large letters. Call the group together and invite each pair to share its answers. For each example, erase a word from the "sin collage" on the board. As each part of the sin collage is erased, erase and open the left side of the circle with *Me* written in it. Continue with examples and the opening of the circle until *Me* is again in a half circle, open to the left toward the circle with *God* written in it.

Ask the teens to think of ways they can say yes to Jesus. Have each teen write one way on the board under the word *Yes.*

Conclude this activity in the following way:

As we heard from Isaiah, God's mercy and forgiveness will wipe away our sins and again open the way for a new relationship. Even though we say no to God and turn away through our words and actions, Paul reminds us in the second reading that God is never anything but yes to us. Our yes in return restores and renews our relationship with God.

Consider giving the teens a button or sticker that says, "Say *yes* to God," to remember this session.

Activity Ideas The following activity ideas also relate to the Scripture readings. You may want to read the passage(s) indicated as part of the activity.

- Invite the teens to create a prayer service around the beautiful words we pray during the Eucharist: "Lord, I am not worthy to receive you, but only say the word and I shall be healed." (Ps. 41:2–3,4–5,13–14)

- Obtain the movie *Jesus of Nazareth* (available from Bridgestone Multimedia, see p. 133 for their address and phone number). Show the clip in which Jesus heals the paralyzed man, as in this week's Gospel reading. Freeze the frame after the men have lowered their friend into the room, but before Jesus heals him. Ask the teens the following questions:
  - How does sin sometimes paralyze us and prevent us from being our true self?
  - How does holding a grudge against another person paralyze us from growing in a relationship?
  - Do you have friends in need of healing that you might recommend to Jesus in prayer?
  Show the rest of the video clip after the discussion. (Mark 2:1–12)

- Compare the prayers used in the sacrament of reconciliation with those used in the sacrament of anointing of the sick. How do these prayers relate to the Gospel reading? (Mark 2:1–12)

- Ask the teens to interview people who minister in pastoral care or have been ministered to. What does the experience mean to them? How do they minister to the physical and spiritual needs of the person? How have they been ministered to in return? (Mark 2:1–12)

Eighth Sunday of the Year

Scripture Readings (84)
- ❖ Hos. 2:16,17,21–22
- ❖ Ps. 103:1–2,3–4,8,10,12–13
- ❖ 2 Cor. 3:1–6
- ❖ Mark 2:18–22

God's Word

A major theme of the Scripture readings is "A covenant of love."

Hosea likens God's love for God's people to the love between a bride and a bridegroom on their honeymoon, where in quietness (the desert) together they speak to each other's hearts. We need not literally go off into the desert to hear God speak to our heart, but we need to make time in our own way for the Lord.

The psalmist lists many of the wonderful attributes and good works of a kind and merciful God, and calls on the people to bless and praise this God who has given the precious gift of love.

Paul tells the Corinthians that God's covenant of love, established through the gift of the Son, Jesus, is written on their hearts and displayed by their lives. He says that this covenant goes beyond written laws, rules, and regulations, and it is fully realized in the Spirit.

Mark's Gospel shows the tension between the old and the new. The Pharisees want Jesus to hold onto old traditions and laws. Jesus uses cloth and wineskins to teach the Pharisees that these laws can rightfully be broken in order to celebrate Jesus, who is God's covenant present with them.

Themes for Teens

The following themes from the Scriptures relate to the lives of teens:
- God speaks to our heart.
- God's spirit is the source of the good we do.
- The goodness of God is all around us and in us.
- We must be open to God making all things new.
- God's love is our promise.

Our Response

Activity Your Life as a Letter of Christ

This activity is keyed to the second reading and the challenge it poses. It invites the teens to look at their life as if they are a letter written by Jesus.

Make available to the teens a variety of stationery or note cards for letter writing. Arrange for a setting in which they are assured of quiet, with plenty of room to spread out and work on their own.

Give everyone a copy of 2 Cor. 3:1–6. Ask them to read it to themselves and reflect on this question: If you are a letter of Christ, what do you say with your life? Direct them to respond to the question in letter form. Allow at least 30 minutes for this activity. You may want to tell the teens that the letter need not be shared. Urge them to write more with their heart than with their head.

Activity Ideas   The following activity ideas also relate to the Scripture readings. You may want to read the passage(s) indicated as part of the activity.

- After reading together the passage from Hosea, ask the teens to share about a time when they did what they thought was just and right even though it might not have been the popular choice. Brainstorm some ways to build courage when faced with tough choices. (Hos. 2:16–17,21–22)

- Pray the responsorial psalm together, with a different teen reading each verse. Then divide the teens into small groups and give each group a pencil and a sheet of paper. Challenge them, without looking at the psalm, to list as many of the adjectives used to describe God that they can remember. Invite them to add their own adjectives to describe God and share these with the large group. (Ps. 103:1–2,3–4,8,10,12–13)

- Ahead of time, ask the teens to locate copies of several newspapers from twenty-five to thirty years ago. Have them compare and contrast the news stories, ads, technology, prices, issues, and fads with a newspaper from today. How many old ways of doing things have been replaced with new ways? Ask the teens how this activity can help them understand what Jesus is telling us about how the old and new cannot always exist together. (Mark 2:18–22)

- Have the young people make mobiles with Psalm 103 written on the top. On each part that hangs down, tell them to illustrate one of God's many blessings recounted in the psalm. Hang the mobiles in the commons of your worship space or a school corridor. (Ps. 103:1–2,3–4,8,10,12–13)

- Ask the teens to compare a legal contract between two parties with a marriage covenant between two people. Make sure that the differences between an agreement and mutual promises are discussed. Also discuss the difference between the binding force in a legal contract (sanctions) and that in a marriage covenant (commitment and faithfulness). (All readings)

Ninth Sunday of the Year

Scripture Readings
(87)
- ❖ Deut. 5:12–15
- ❖ Ps. 81:3–4,5–6,6–8,10–11
- ❖ 2 Cor. 4:6–11
- ❖ Mark 2:23—3:6

God's Word   A major theme of the Scripture readings is "Keep holy the Sabbath."
All the readings, and especially Deuteronomy, call to mind the commandment "Keep holy the Sabbath day." This commandment is an expression of God's compassion for the overburdened and those enslaved in labor. Everyone is to be guaranteed a weekly day of rest, on which God's compassion is celebrated and praised. If Sunday has become like every other day of the week, it is not meant to be that way. Six days of the week are for work and study. The seventh day is reserved for making more time for the welfare of others and for celebrating God's compassion for us.

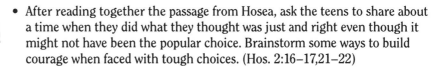

The psalmist finds joy in God's compassion and calls on us to sing God's praises. Even though we might not use a timbrel, lyre, or harp to praise God, our words and actions become instruments for playing and rejoicing in God's goodness.

Instead of attributing his successes to himself, Paul acknowledges the power of God in his mortal, fragile body as the real reason for his accomplishments.

In Mark's Gospel, the Pharisees get hung up on the rules and regulations about what can and cannot be done on the Sabbath. Jesus sets them straight on the real meaning of the day—a willingness to be open to God's compassion for people and to reach out to those in need.

These readings ask some tough questions: How is our Sunday different from the other days of our week? Do we spend more time with our family, read the Scriptures together, rest from our work, reflect on how we can show God's compassion to people in need? Do we celebrate God at Mass on Sunday? Do we gather with our youth group to celebrate and remember God's love?

Themes for Teens   The following themes from the Scriptures relate to the lives of teens:
- Make time for God.
- Make time for extending God's compassion.
- Restore the Lord's day.
- Jesus puts people before rules.
- Praise God in words and actions.

Our Response

Activity   Make the Lord's Day Special

This community project connects with all the readings. It helps build awareness of the importance of making time for God and God's compassion in our life, and of inspiring a renewed reverence for the Lord's day.

Tell the teens to imagine they work for a large national advertising agency, and their task is to promote making time for God and God's compassion in people's lives. They are assigned to promote the slogan, "Make the Lord's day special."

Give them some examples to start with, such as these:
- Make a top 10 list of reasons to go to Mass on Sunday. Post the list in your school or parish and publish it in the youth group newsletter.
- Make buttons or design T-shirts with the slogan, "Make the Lord's day special."
- Plan a prayer service or a retreat on the theme and lead it for another group of teens.
- Sponsor a school or parish contest for the best essay, song, or poem about this theme.
- Plan ways to help people who need Sunday as a day of rest and recreation. For example, baby-sit for young parents who work all week, visit an elderly person who is alone, and so on.

After the teens plan their advertising strategy, challenge them to put it into action. If you are doing this in the parish, recruit other groups— younger and older—to take part in the campaign.

Activity Ideas

The following activity ideas also relate to the Scripture readings. You may want to read the passage(s) indicated as part of the activity.

- Spark a discussion with this question: If we give God only one hour at Mass on Sunday and the rest of the day is like any other, are we really keeping holy the Lord's day? What can we do to keep the day holy? Challenge the teens to take this question home to their family to share ideas and set some goals together. (Deut. 5:12–15; Mark 2:23—3:6)

- Have the teens write a prayer service around the theme "Excuses, excuses." Alternate short vignettes in which the teens portray reasons for skipping Mass, such as staying up too late the night before or going to a sports event, with passages from the Scriptures in which Jesus took time to pray, to teach others to pray, or to talk with his father. (Deut. 5:12–15; Mark 2:23—3:6)

- Encourage the teens to start a journal and make time at least once a week to converse with God or reflect on the Scriptures. Challenge them to think of other ways they can set aside time in their day for God and for others. (Deut. 5:12–15; Mark 2:23—3:6)

- Invite the young people to share stories of family traditions or things their family does to make Sunday special. Tell them to ask their parents, grandparents, and other adults to share their recollections and why these times were important to them. (Deut. 5:12–15; Mark 2:23—3:6)

Tenth Sunday of the Year

Scripture Readings (90)

- ❖ Gen. 3:9–15
- ❖ Ps. 130:1–2,3–4,5–6,7–8
- ❖ 2 Cor. 4:13—5:1
- ❖ Mark 3:20–35

God's Word

A major theme of the Scripture readings is "Making choices between good and evil in our life."

In Genesis we hear about how Adam and Eve made a bad choice. Adam blamed it on Eve. Eve blamed it on the snake. But they used their free will to oppose what they knew to be God's will, and they had to live with the consequences—getting kicked out of paradise. This story is often told to explain why there is evil in the world.

The psalm calls upon the mercy of God and expresses assurance of redemption.

Paul tells us that if we truly have faith, we will be required to speak out and share that faith. He also says that it is not what is outside our body that counts or that reveals who we are. Rather, it is what is unseen—God's spirit—that lasts forever. If we choose to seek God, we have the promise of heaven to look forward to.

In the Gospel of Mark, Jesus includes his followers as members of his family. He is not putting down or diminishing his own family. Rather, he expands the meaning of family. He tells us that all those who do God's will are his brothers and sisters.

Ordinary Time

<table>
<tr><td>Themes for Teens</td><td>The following themes from the Scriptures relate to the lives of teens:</td></tr>
</table>

Themes for Teens

The following themes from the Scriptures relate to the lives of teens:

- God gives us the freedom to make our own choices.
- Sin has its consequences.
- God forgives our sins.
- We are Jesus' brothers and sisters.
- If you have faith, you have to share it.

Our Response

Activity

Lead Us Not into Temptation

This prayer service is keyed to the psalm. It combines messages from modern music with messages from traditional prayer (the Lord's Prayer and the Psalms) to acknowledge sin in our world and to seek God's help in dealing with it.

Before the prayer service, ask the teens to search their music collections for messages of sin in our world. You may want to divide the teens into five groups and direct each group to come up with a different song. Each song should highlight a different sin in our society. Tell the groups to bring their song with them the next time you meet. They should have the song queued up and ready to play, and be prepared to play only part of the song.

Order of Prayer

- *Call to prayer.*

    All: Our Father
    who is in heaven,
    holy is your name.
    Your kingdom come.
    Your will be done
    on earth as it is in heaven.
    Give us this day our daily bread
    and forgive us our sins,
    as we forgive those who sin against us.

- Play a snippet of each of the five songs. After each song, have the teens respond, "With the Lord there is mercy and fullness of redemption." Then pause for quiet reflection on the need for forgiveness in our own life. End by praying together, "And lead us not into temptation, but deliver us from evil."

Activity Ideas

The following activity ideas also relate to the Scripture readings. You may want to read the passage(s) indicated as part of the activity.

- Use an apple as a discussion starter. Toss the apple around the group. The first person to catch the apple gives an example of one way the devil tempts us. The next person who catches the apple describes a way to avoid or resist that temptation. Continue tossing the apple and keeping the discussion going until all have had a chance to contribute. (Gen. 3:9–15)

- Direct the teens to write in their journal about one of the toughest temptations they face right now. Tell them to write a prayer asking God's help to deal with the temptation in a positive, constructive way. (Gen. 3:9–15; Ps. 130:1–2,3–4,5–6,7–8)

- Start a discussion with this question: How does the devil use peer pressure to tempt us to sin? Ask the teens to brainstorm practical strategies they can use to resist temptation. (Gen. 3:9–15; Ps. 130:1–2,3–4,5–6,7–8)

- Invite a priest to chat with the teens in an informal session about the sacrament of reconciliation. Often young people have questions, fears, and misconceptions about the sacrament and will welcome a chance to talk candidly about them. (Ps. 130:1–2,3–4,5–6,7–8)

- Jesus calls us beyond blood and kinship relations in the doing of God's will. Direct the teens to name some of the ways God calls us to reach beyond family and friends to do God's will. (All readings)

Eleventh Sunday of the Year

Scripture Readings (93)
- ❖ Ezek. 17:22–24
- ❖ Ps. 92:2–3,13–14,15–16
- ❖ 2 Cor. 5:6–10
- ❖ Mark 4:26–34

God's Word

A major theme of the Scripture readings is "Sowing seeds of faith."

All the readings portray God as the sower of seeds—the seeds of faith. Ezekiel sees God as the planter of a new seed (tender shoot) that will become a great tree—a new king that will rule his people.

The psalmist gives thanks to the Lord for the Lord's goodness. Rooted in the Lord, a person will bear fruit to a ripe old age. Bearing fruit with our life means more than just existing, or taking up space. Living for others and sharing faith enables us to bear fruit for the Lord.

In Second Corinthians, Paul talks about making it an aim to please the Lord, and about the importance of trusting in God rather than in what we do or what we can see.

Mark tells us that the people wanted Jesus to explain the Reign of God. They were having trouble understanding, so Jesus used the image of the mustard seed. If a seed as tiny as a mustard seed can grow into a mighty tree, then, too, one act of faith can grow into a lifetime of believing. It is okay to have doubts or to worry that our faith is not strong enough. If we allow Jesus to nourish our faith and if we nourish our faith, it will grow and touch many in our parish and family.

Hope and patience also run through all these readings. Each time a seed is planted and a plant emerges, we experience a miracle. So, too, our faith is a miracle. Faith takes root and grows slowly with hidden and mysterious nourishment from God, even when we are unaware of it. Patience is needed by all who wait for the Reign of God.

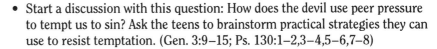

Themes for Teens   The following themes from the Scriptures relate to the lives of teens:
- Root your faith in the Lord.
- Walk by faith.
- The Reign of God is growing.
- Faith grows slowly.
- God sows the seeds of our faith.

Our Response

Activity   Walking by Faith

This game and discussion activity is keyed to the reading from Second Corinthians. It offers the teens an opportunity to reflect on the difficulty of walking by faith rather than sight. It stresses the importance of learning to trust in God to lead us through the times when we feel as though we are blindfolded.

Direct a volunteer to leave the room. While that person is gone, create an obstacle course using chairs, tables, and other available materials, so that the person will have to walk around, climb under, or go through a variety of obstacles. Outside the room, blindfold the volunteer. When she or he comes into the room, ask her or him to follow directions through the obstacle course. Invite the other teens to take turns giving directions to guide the volunteer through the obstacles.

Read 2 Cor. 5:6–10 aloud. Pose the following questions to the person who went through the obstacle course:
- Why was it tough to go through the obstacle course blindfolded?
- Was it hard to trust that others would guide you through?

Pose these questions to the entire group:
- Why is it hard to go where God is leading us when we don't know what God has in store?
- Why is it sometimes hard to trust in God and have faith that God will do the best for us?
- How do we react when others challenge our faith and demand proof before they will believe what we believe?
- Which of Jesus' disciples had trouble believing in Jesus without proof?
- How does the experience of being blindfolded relate to the Scripture reading?

Activity Ideas   The following activity ideas also relate to the Scripture readings. You may want to read the passage(s) indicated as part of the activity.

- Ask the teens to name the fruits of the Holy Spirit. If they get stuck, fill in the remaining ones. The fruits are love, kindness, joy, peace, patience, generosity, faithfulness, gentleness, self-control, goodness, suffering, and chastity. Read Psalm 92 aloud. Then divide the teens into groups of four and direct each group to pick one of the fruits and give an example of one way they can bear that fruit in their life. Consider having a fruit salad ready to share after the discussion. (Ps. 92:2–3,13–14,15–16)

- Invite a newly baptized adult Catholic to give a witness talk about his or her faith journey—particularly about how people planted the seeds of faith in him or her and how others helped that faith grow. (Mark 4:26–34)

- Plant real flower seeds and the seeds of faith by making small planters to give as gifts to shut-ins or hospitalized members of your parish community. Decorate the planters with snippets from this week's readings. (All readings)

- Plant a tree on the parish property or a flower bed outside your school. Read one of today's Scripture passages between each part of the project—digging, planting, and watering. Have a discussion afterward about what a plant needs in order to grow and what our faith needs for it to grow. (All readings)

Twelfth Sunday of the Year

Scripture Readings (96)

- ❖ Job 38:1:8–11
- ❖ Ps. 107:23–24,25–26,28–29,30–31
- ❖ 2 Cor. 5:14–17
- ❖ Mark 4:35–41

God's Word

A major theme of the Scripture readings is "Seeking safety in the storm."

Job, who was once rich and prosperous, finds himself sick and destitute. His family has even been killed. Job demands an answer from God about why such terrible things have happened to him. As an answer, Job learns that he is dealing with a God of mighty power—a God who sets limits on the limitless sea.

The psalmist also uses the sea to give examples of God's power. When God commands the sea to toss its waves, it does; when God hushes the wind, it becomes a gentle breeze. The psalmist describes how those who sail the seas for a living depend on God. They have seen firsthand God's might, and they call on God for protection.

Paul, too, speaks of God's power—the power of God's love conveyed to everyone in the love of Jesus, a power that makes everyone a new creation. To accept this love and to live in the love of Christ requires a radically different outlook. We can no longer see ourselves and others as merely human, but as new creations embraced in the love of God.

The Gospel again uses the might of the sea and the wind to illustrate the power of God manifested in Jesus Christ. All of us get caught in storms in our own life. But with faith in Jesus we can pass safely through the midst of them.

Themes for Teens

The following themes from the Scriptures relate to the lives of teens:
- God is our hope in the storm.
- When God speaks, the waves listen.
- Jesus makes all things new.
- Jesus is our protector.
- God rescues those in danger.

Ordinary Time

Our Response

Activity   God's Help in the Storm

This activity is keyed to the Gospel reading. It calls for an older teen or young adult to talk about the importance of turning to Jesus during the stormy times in life. If you ask an adult, urge that person to draw on her or his experiences as a youth in sharing this talk with the teens. You may want to incorporate the Gospel reading into the talk.

The following questions are designed to help the speaker flesh out the important points:

1. Describe some of the storms in your life.
- Have you had problems with grades, relationships, dealing with your family, peer pressure, and the like?
- Have you ever felt like you were the only one going through that problem?
- What were some of the feelings you had?
- If you feel comfortable doing so, share one specific example of a tough storm in your life.

2. Strategies for getting through storms.
- What were some of the strategies you used to get through life's storms?
- Who were some of the people who helped you? Who can we turn to when we need help? [You may want to get audience participation here.]
- What are some things you can do to help yourself get through storms?

3. God is our comfort amidst the storm.
- How did God help you get through some of the tough times in your life?
- How can prayer be a source of comfort in the storm?
- What are some different ways to pray?

4. Miracles are for everyone.
- Jesus did not work miracles only for those who lived in his time.
- How has Jesus worked miracles in your life through other people?
- How does God work miracles through you?

General Tips

- Give the talk to one person and seek feedback before giving it to the entire group.
- Speak slowly and thoughtfully.
- Maintain eye contact with your audience.
- Give personal examples and share stories from your own life.
- Use humor, music, poems, prayers, or symbols to help make your point.
- Limit your talk to 15 to 20 minutes.
- Be yourself.

Activity Ideas

The following activity ideas also relate to the Scripture readings. You may want to read the passage(s) indicated as part of the activity.

- Spend some time talking about miracles with your teens. What is a miracle? Send them to the Scriptures to find other examples of miracles. How did Jesus use miracles to teach the Good News? (Mark 4:35–41)

- Miracles are often classified into four groups: healings, exorcisms, resuscitations, and nature miracles. Direct the teens to reread today's Gospel passage and classify the miracle in it. Challenge them to give examples of other miracles. (Mark 4:35–41)

- Pose this question for a journal-writing activity: After Jesus calmed the storm, he asked the disciples, "'Why are you terrified? Why are you lacking in faith?'" What are some of the things that cause your faith to be shaken? (Mark 4:35–41)

- Divide the teens into small groups and ask them to reread the Gospel. Next, send each group to a separate place and ask the participants to create a skit that recreates, in a modern setting, the Apostles' experience on the Sea of Galilee. (The setting doesn't have to involve a windstorm, but can be any situation in which faith in God's power is needed to sustain hope.) Invite the teens to share their skits with the entire group. (Mark 4:35–41)

Thirteenth Sunday of the Year

Scripture Readings (99)

❖ Wis. 1:13–15; 2:23–24
❖ Ps. 30:2,4,5–6,11,12,13
❖ 2 Cor. 8:7,9,13–15
❖ Mark 5:21–24,35–43

God's Word

A major theme of the Scripture readings is "God's healing touch."

The first reading from Wisdom disputes the commonly held belief that when death and destruction happen, it must be God's will. Rather, God is seen as a God of life, who gives people a share of divine life and makes them imperishable. To trust in God is to trust that God is a healing God who brings life out of death. To not trust in God is to see life ending in destruction and in effect to believe as Satan would have us believe.

The psalmist praises the Lord, who rescues him from "those going down into the pit." The psalm is hopeful, and even though weeping and sadness are part of the night, dawn comes, and with it, rejoicing. With God on our side, we can leave mourning behind and dance once again.

Paul's words can be read in light of the goodness of God proclaimed in the first reading. Those of us who believe in and share in the gift of immortality given to us in Jesus' Resurrection should be moved to share our mortal gifts with those in need. Charity is the call of every Christian.

The Gospel relates two powerful stories of healing—Jesus curing the woman who suffers bleeding, and his raising to life the daughter of Jairus. Both stories reveal the intent of God to rescue us from our mortality and the healing power of God's touch and of our touching God in Jesus. Both the woman and Jairus reach out to Jesus for what he has to share—the healing power of God. The woman is cured by her touching of Jesus with the faith that he could make her well.

Ordinary Time

Themes for Teens   The following themes from the Scriptures relate to the lives of teens:
- Our God is a God of life, not death.
- If you are rich in faith, be rich in mercy.
- The touch of Jesus heals.
- Take your needs to the Lord.
- Have faith and God will heal you.
- We are called to share our wealth with those in need.

Our Response

Activity   ## The Gift of Touch

This activity is keyed to the Gospel reading. It invites the teens to reflect on how God has touched their life through the touch of other people.

Gather the teens in a circle and give each a copy of the poem "Touch." Number and highlight the sentences or phrases, and have the teens take turns reading them.

> "Touch"
> I'm thankful, Lord, for the touch of a friend's hand,
>   for the hug of sympathy and friendly warmth,
>   for the embrace of love and care.
> I'm thankful for the people whose lives touch
>   mine with friendship.
> I recall, Lord, the touch of the hands that helped
>   me grow from childhood to this day:
> The touch of parents and friends that meant
>   security and love;
> The touch of a friend whose presence cheered me
>   when I was sad;
> The touch of encouragement when I was afraid;
> The touch of sympathy when I was unhappy.
> I thank you, Lord, for this gift;
> You have touched me many times with
>   your own presence
> Through the goodness of others.
>
> I remember the touches that wounded me,
> That still smart in my memory;
> Help me to forgive the lasting sting of hurt,
>   insult or rejection.
>
> Help me, Lord, to use this gift in your service,
> To nurture your love among us.
> Let me not exploit the loneliness
>   and vulnerability of others;
> Let my touch be a touch of care, compassion
>   and kindness;
> Let it be a touch of joy and freedom;
> And in all touches, embraces and precious
>   moments of warmth,
> Let me remember that I am meeting one made
>   from love,
> In the image and likeness of a loving God.
>
> Thank you, Lord, for the gift of touch.

(Neary, *The Calm Beneath the Storm*, pp. 10–11)

90

Ask the teens to pair up and discuss the following questions:

- How has Jesus touched you through other people?
- How has Jesus touched others through you?

Then discuss the answers as a whole group. After the discussion, invite the teens to join in shared prayer, thanking God for someone who has touched their life and touched off God's healing power in them. As each person offers a prayer, invite him or her to grasp the hand of the person next to him or her, until all are united in prayer and by touch.

Activity Ideas The following activity ideas also relate to the Scripture readings. You may want to read the passage(s) indicated as part of the activity.

- Ask the teens to bring in a week's worth of newspapers and clip out all the bad things that happened in their community, nation, and world that week. Pose these questions for discussion:
  - What are some of the causes of evil in the world?
  - Why is it tough to understand why so many bad things happen to good people?

  Read the first reading together. Ask the young people what they learned from the reading. (Wis. 1:13–15; 2:23–24)

- Travel to a nearby gravel pit or construction site where all the teens can gather together in a pit. (Make sure you get permission at the construction site.) Read the responsorial psalm together, alternating boys and girls for each verse. Ask the teens to share answers to these questions:
  - When have you felt like you were stuck in a pit?
  - How did you get out of it? How did others help you out? How did God help you out?

  Conclude by linking hands and helping one another out of the pit. (Ps. 30:2,4,5–6,11,12,13)

- Send the teens out with cameras to capture photos of some parish members who have touched their life in a special way. Create an honor roll picture gallery in the commons or vestibule of your church. (Mark 5:21–24,35–43)

- Direct the teens to read the second reading at home with their family and to pose the question: Do we as a family share our wealth to help the needy? Challenge the teens and their families to map out a month-by-month action plan for reaching out to the needy in their community. (2 Cor. 8:7,9,13–15)

Fourteenth Sunday of the Year

Scripture Readings (102)
- ❖ Ezek. 2:2–5
- ❖ Ps. 123:1–2,2,3–4
- ❖ 2 Cor. 12:7–10
- ❖ Mark 6:1–6

God's Word

A major theme of the Scriptures readings is "Being a prophet isn't easy."

In Ezekiel, we learn that God sends prophets both to stubborn people and to those who accept them. Prophets do not always get a warm reception. God may not set us on our feet, as with Ezekiel, but we can be sure that God is calling us to be a prophet in some way, shape, or form.

The psalmist says that everyone should fix their eyes on the Lord. This is really tough to do with all the distractions in our life. If we just pay attention, we can learn a lot by watching Jesus and following his ways.

The reading from Second Corinthians finds Paul experiencing the vulnerability involved in proclaiming and witnessing the word of God. In this experience he realizes what appears to be a contradiction. Paul says that when he is weak, then he is strong. In fact, Paul finds his weakness leaves more room for the power of Christ to have its way. This way of being counters a society that encourages us to be as humanly powerful as we can, to think of ourselves first, and to not worry about what happens to others. Those who are to be prophets need to keep this in mind.

In Mark's Gospel, Jesus journeys home to find that prophets are not usually welcome in their hometown. The people back home focus only on Jesus' roots as a carpenter's son and miss the point—the Good News of God's salvation. Real prophets take a beating, but they stick to what they believe. They don't bend to peer pressure and change their beliefs just because others think they should.

Themes for Teens

The following themes from the Scriptures relate to the lives of teens:
- God speaks to us through prophets.
- Fix your eyes on the Lord.
- The Spirit can stand you on your feet.
- Even Jesus got rejected sometimes.
- There is strength in weakness.
- Prophets stand firm in their convictions, even in the face of rejection.

Our Response

Activity

The Eyes Have It

This activity is keyed to the responsorial psalm and the need to keep our eyes fixed on the Lord. It starts with an exercise on paying attention and leads to a discussion on ways we are distracted from fixing our eyes on the Lord.

Before the teens arrive, put a collection of about thirty items on a table in the center of your gathering space. They can range from a stapler and a book to a quarter and a paper clip. Do not draw attention to the objects as the teens enter the room. After they have been in the room for 5 minutes, cover the table with a cloth. Ask the teens to write down as many objects as they can remember. Lift up the cloth and let the teens see how well they did. Direct one of the teens to read Ps. 123:1–2,2,3–4.

Encourage the teens to discuss the following questions:
- What does the psalm tell us about paying attention?
- What did this activity teach us about paying attention?
- Why is it important to keep our eyes fixed on the Lord?
- What might we miss if we are not paying attention?
- What are some of the people and things that distract us from fixing our eyes on the Lord?

Note in closing that prophets fix their attention both on God and on the way people are relating to one another. Their role is to call attention to instances when God's ways are not being followed by people in their relationships with one another.

Activity Ideas   The following activity ideas also relate to the Scripture readings. You may want to read the passage(s) indicated as part of the activity.

- Direct the teens to do some research on the life of Mother Teresa, a modern prophet. Discuss how her life embodies the message of the second reading. (2 Cor. 12:7–10)

- Here are some questions for journal writing:
  - How do you think Jesus felt when he was rejected?
  - How did Jesus deal with rejection?
  - How do you feel when you are rejected?
  - How do you deal with rejection?
  - Have you ever rejected someone else?
  - How can we avoid rejecting others?

(Mark 6:1–6)

- Take close-up photographs of the faces of all the teens in your group. Cut out only the eyes and post them on a sheet of poster board. As a fun lead-in to a discussion on the responsorial psalm, allow the teens to try and guess who owns each set of eyes. (Ps. 123:1–2,2,3–4)

- Ask the teens to state several moral issues they have to deal with. Then take a poll on where they stand on these issues, but instead of using a handout, have them indicate their position by standing in the corner of the room labeled with a sign that corresponds to their position: "Agree," "Disagree," or "No Opinion." For discussion, ask them what happened when they acted like a prophet and stuck to what they believed about issues such as these—when they didn't bend to peer pressure and change their beliefs or behavior just because others thought they should. (Mark 6:1–6)

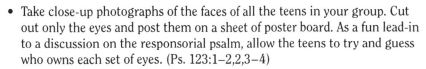

Fifteenth Sunday of the Year

Scripture Readings (105)

- ❖ Amos 7:12–15
- ❖ Ps. 85:9–10,11–12,13–14
- ❖ Eph. 1:3–14
- ❖ Mark 6:7–13

God's Word

A major theme of the Scripture readings is "We are chosen and sent forth."

Amos tells us that the call to be a prophet can come to anyone. Amos was just a shepherd when God called him. Commitment is much more important than credentials.

Psalm 85 echoes the main message of the prophets: a call to works of peace and justice.

In Ephesians, we hear again that we have been chosen by God. The entire reading is a list of blessings. God gives each of us a special blessing to share.

In the Gospel reading, the Apostles are sent forth. Jesus didn't give the Apostles time to pack. He told them to waste no time getting about their mission. Perhaps, for us, this is also a call from Jesus to embrace a simple lifestyle in an age of overindulgence. We also must shed those things that prevent us from doing God's work and leave them behind as we share the Good News.

Themes for Teens

The following themes from the Scriptures relate to the lives of teens:

- God has called you.
- You are part of God's plan.
- Share your blessings.
- Our mission is to serve.
- We are all God's messengers.

Our Response

Activity

  Prayer Service

This activity is keyed to the reading from the Letter to the Ephesians. It is a prayer service and will take some preparation. Teach the opening song to the teens before the prayer service if they are not familiar with it. If one of your young people plays piano or guitar, invite him or her to accompany you.

Make a copy of the reading from Ephesians and replace each use of the word *us* in the reading with one or two of your teens' names. Make sure all the teens' names are included.

Discuss the role of blessings in our life and in our church. You may want to show them the *Book of Blessings,* by the International Commission on English in the Liturgy, and allow them to read a few of the blessings. Talk about how we can be blessings for one another.

Put all the teens' names in a bag and have them each draw a name. Ask them to write a one-sentence blessing for that person and to be prepared to read it during the prayer. After the prayer, they can give it to that person as a gift.

Conduct the following prayer service:

- *Call to prayer.*

- *Opening song.* "God Has Chosen Me," by Bernadette Farrell, vv. 1 and 2 (*Today's Missal, Music Issue, 1993* [Portland: Oregon Catholic Press], no. 619)

- *Reading.* Eph. 1:3–14, with the names of teens inserted

- *Sharing of one-sentence blessings.*

- *General blessing.*
  All. May the Lord bless you and keep you.
  May the Lord always be with you.
  May you learn to walk in the Lord's ways.
  Amen.

- *Closing song.* "God Has Chosen Me" by Bernadette Farrell, vv. 1 and 2

Activity Ideas

The following activity ideas also relate to the Scripture readings. You may want to read the passage(s) indicated as part of the activity.

- The following questions can be used for journal writing:
  ○ Is God calling you to be a prophet?
  ○ How does it make you feel to know that God chose you for something special even before you were born?

(Amos 7:12–15)

- Ask the teens to print their name in big block letters on a half sheet of poster board. Hang the posters around your classroom or meeting space. Encourage the teens to affirm one another by writing down some of each person's gifts and talents on his or her poster. Stress that the things they write *must* be positive. (Eph. 1:3–14)

- Ask everyone coming to your next meeting or class to bring an empty suitcase with them. Read Mark 6:7–13, pointing out that Jesus told his disciples not to take anything with them on their journey. Use the suitcases as a springboard for a discussion on the things we need to unpack or the baggage we need to dispose of before we can really follow Jesus. (Mark 6:7–13)

- Collect an assortment of stuff that is part of teens' lives. Some examples: in-line skates, a CD, a football, a telephone, a can of soda, makeup, a pair of designer jeans. Direct each teen to choose one item from the pile and talk about how "stuff" sometimes gets in the way of living a Christian life. Ask why Jesus told the Apostles not to take anything with them. Talk about how the Apostles' stuff would have weighed them down. (Mark 6:7–13)

Sixteenth Sunday of the Year

Scripture Readings (108)

❖ Jer. 23:1–6
❖ Ps. 23:1–3,3–4,5,6
❖ Eph. 2:13–18
❖ Mark 6:30–34

God's Word

A major theme of the Scripture readings is "Come rest awhile."

Through Jeremiah, God warns the shepherds who divide and scatter the sheep. God will gather those sheep together who were not cared for before and find a good shepherd to look after them. This good shepherd is a "shoot of David," which many biblical scholars see as an allusion to the coming of Jesus and the fulfillment of God's promise to David to continue his line of descendants.

The psalmist describes the Lord God as a good shepherd. He gives a job description for a good shepherd as one who provides for green pastures and restful waters, who shows the path to walk and gives courage in the dark valley, who calls people to the table and invites them to live in the Lord's house. This psalm is a personal favorite of many people because it is a prayer for comfort and protection.

The passage from Ephesians says that Christ not only brings peace, but he *is* peace. Like a shepherd who draws his flock together, Jesus draws us together into one community so that we are not alone, but one with others. Where there is hostility, Jesus brings reconciliation and peace.

The Gospel reading shows us that even Jesus and the Apostles needed a break now and then. Yet people kept coming to them. But even when he was tired, Jesus, like a good shepherd, had compassion for those who were in need. He saw the people as sheep without a shepherd, as in the first reading.

Themes for Teens

The following themes from the Scriptures relate to the lives of teens:
- Jesus is the Good Shepherd.
- Watch out for those who scatter the sheep.
- Christ *is* peace.
- Jesus and his followers needed to rest now and then to refresh themselves for compassionate loving.
- Make time for quiet in your life.
- Be compassionate, as Jesus was.

Our Response

Activity

Unexpected Quiet

This quiet reflection activity is keyed to the Gospel reading. It invites the teens to accept Jesus' invitation to "'Come by yourselves to an out-of-the-way place and rest a little.'"

Before the teens arrive, arrange your regular meeting space in an entirely different way. For example, dim the lights; play quiet, soothing music in the background; put comfortable cushions on the floor to sit on. You might even consider meeting in a different place if possible.

When the teens arrive, greet them one at a time. Give them a Bible and a copy of the following instructions. Allow 20 minutes for this part of the activity.

- Be very still. Be very quiet. Do not speak at all after receiving these instructions.
- Find a quiet place to sit by yourself. Do not sit near anyone. Do not say a word to anyone.
- Read the Scripture passage marked in your Bible: Mark 6:30–34.
- Close your eyes and reflect on the reading.
- Read the Scripture passage again.
- Close your eyes and pray about the reading.
- Remain quiet until you receive further instructions.
  Next, ask the teens to find a partner and discuss this question:
- How did the Scripture passage speak to you in the silence?
  In groups of four, answer the following questions:
- Did you find it tough to be quiet for so long? Why or why not?
- Why is it difficult to find quiet time in our everyday life?
  Draw the entire group together and ask:
- Why is it important for us to accept Jesus' invitation to come away by ourselves to an out-of-the-way place and rest awhile?
- What can you do to make more space for quiet time in your everyday life?

Activity Ideas

The following activity ideas also relate to the Scripture readings. You may want to read the passage(s) indicated as part of the activity.

- Challenge the teens to plan an evening retreat, using each verse of the psalm as a theme for each session. Or use each of the three readings and the psalm as themes for the retreat. (Ps. 23:1–3,3–4,5,6 or all readings)

- Ask the teens to make bookmarks featuring Psalm 23 to give to parish shut-ins or to make handmade sympathy cards to send to teens who have a family member or close friend who has died. (Ps. 23:1–3,3–4,5,6)

- Pray Psalm 23 as a group. Share answers to these questions in pairs: How does this psalm offer you comfort? Why do you think it is one of the most popular psalms? (Ps. 23:1–3,3–4,5,6)

- One name for Jesus is the Good Shepherd. Divide the teens into teams and ask them to brainstorm as many other names for Jesus as they can. Start a discussion on the name they think is most fitting for Jesus and why. (Jer. 23:1–6)

- One main quality of a good shepherd is compassion, especially for those in need. Instruct the teens to relate the need to rest awhile with the energy needed to be compassionate. (Mark 6:30–34)

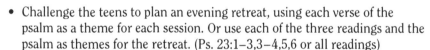

Seventeenth Sunday of the Year

Scripture Readings (111)

- ❖ 2 Kings 4:42–44
- ❖ Ps. 145:10–11,15–16,17–18
- ❖ Eph. 4:1–6
- ❖ John 6:1–15

God's Word

A major theme of the Scripture readings is "Food for body and soul."

In today's readings, we learn that those who trust in the Lord, who have faith in him, will not go hungry. Jesus will give us what we need for both our body and our spirit.

In the Second Book of Kings, a man brings the prophet Elisha twenty barley loaves. The servant protests when Elisha asks him to give what he has to the people to eat, but he follows instructions and, as the Lord said, "'"They shall eat and there shall be some left over."'" God miraculously multiplied the loaves.

The responsorial psalm links the first reading and the Gospel reading. The psalmist rejoices in the hand of the Lord, who satisfies our physical need for food as well as our deeper, spiritual needs. At the same time, the psalm portrays God as approachable, with open hands. It promises that our hungers will be filled in due season.

The Letter to the Ephesians is a prayer for the gifts needed to be a Christian. It is also a small creed—a statement of belief. The writer says we should follow Christ with humility, meekness, and patience, bearing one another lovingly. His creed professes faith in the unity of God—one Father, one Lord, one Spirit—and faith in one baptism, a call to all Christians to be united in faith and service.

In the Gospel reading, Jesus multiplies the loaves and fishes. Jesus begins the day by preaching and teaching—nourishing people's spiritual hunger for the word of God. Later, he fills their physical needs. As in the first reading, the amount of food in the beginning is minimal, but no one goes hungry. They have more than enough to eat—a symbol of the abundance of spiritual food.

Before feeding the hungry people, Jesus blesses the bread and shares it—anticipating what is celebrated as the Eucharist today. At the table of the Eucharist, we receive nourishment for our body and our spirit.

Themes for Teens

The following themes from the Scriptures relate to the lives of teens:
- God gives us what we need.
- When we are hungry, God feeds us.
- Our God is number one.
- Hunger for the Lord.
- We are all part of the Body of Christ.

Our Response

Activity **Baking a Prayer**

This activity is keyed to all the readings. It invites the teens to experience the art of making bread with their own hands and to reflect on the ingredients needed to be a good Christian.

Choose a basic bread recipe from any handy cookbook. Depending on time, you may want to choose a quick-bread recipe that does not require yeast and a lot of time for rising. These can often be prepared in one bowl. (No bread machines allowed.)

Ask the teens: What ingredients are needed to make bread? As they add these ingredients, direct them also to reflect on the ingredients needed to make ourselves into good Christians. Make sure everyone has a part in making the bread and, if possible, use small bread pans so that there will be a separate small loaf for each teen.

As the bread is baking, divide the teens into four groups. Assign each group one of the three readings or the psalm. Ask them to answer the following questions: What message do you find in this reading? How does it connect to our bread-making project? Invite each small group to share its responses with the large group.

During a period of quiet time, direct each teen to compose a short prayer for her or his family, using one of the readings as a springboard.

Give the teens each an index card with a hole punched on one end. Have them write today's Scripture references on one side and their family prayer on the other side. When the bread is cool, wrap it in a plastic bag. Put a piece of string (or a wire twist tie) through the hole in the index card and then use the string to tie the bag shut. Urge the teens to share both the bread and the prayer with their family.

Activity Ideas The following activity ideas also relate to the Scripture readings. You may want to read the passage(s) indicated as part of the activity.

- Divide the teens into groups and ask each group to describe a situation that highlights a characteristic that is the opposite of one of Paul's ingredients for a worthy life, for example, pride as the opposite of humility, rudeness as the opposite of meekness, impatience as the opposite of patience, intolerance as the opposite of bearing one another lovingly. Tell the teens to exchange situation cards with another group and brainstorm ways to resolve the situation they are given. (Eph. 4:1–6)

- Give the teens each a piece of paper and a pencil. Instruct them to write down as much of the Sunday creed (profession of faith) as they can remember. Have them do it individually first, and then in small groups, to see how much they remember. Use the following or similar questions for discussion:
  - Why is it important to think about the words we pray every Sunday at Mass?
  - Do you really believe what the words say?

(Eph. 4:1–6)

- Prepare for this activity by asking everyone to bring to the next meeting one ingredient for soup. Make sure you have a soup base to start with.

  Begin by reading the story *Stone Soup,* by Marcia Brown (New York: Aladdin Books, Macmillan Publishing Co., 1947). Ask the teens how the people in the story managed to end up with more than enough to eat.

  Make soup together, using the ingredients each person brought. After making the soup, ask the teens why it was possible for everyone to have a meal when each brought only one small item. How does this relate to today's readings? (2 Kings 4:42–44; Ps. 145:10–11,15–16,17–18; John 6:1–15)

• If you have a bread-making ministry in your parish, contact the person in charge and ask if the teens can help make bread for the Eucharist one week. (2 Kings 4:42–44; Ps. 145:10–11,15–16,17–18; John 6:1–15)

Eighteenth Sunday of the Year

Scripture Readings (114)

❖ Exod. 16:2–4,12–15
❖ Ps. 78:3–4,23–24,25,54
❖ Eph. 4:17,20–24
❖ John 6:24–35

God's Word

A major theme of the Scripture readings is "The Bread of Life."

In all these readings, the people are concerned about filling their physical hunger with bread. They don't seem to recognize their deeper hungers or that bread is a sign of one who can satisfy those hungers.

In the reading from Exodus, the Israelites are experiencing grave doubt. They have forgotten how bad they had it in Egypt, as well as God's miraculous intervention to set them free. They are grumbling about having to rough it in the desert. They lack faith and trust in God. But God hears their complaints and fulfills the promise to take care of them. God answers their physical needs by sending quail and manna, but God's real goal is to increase their faith. God says, "'You shall have your fill of bread, so that you may know that I, the Lord, am your God.'" But even when manna is available, Moses still has to explain that it came from God.

The psalm celebrates the miracle of bread from heaven and foreshadows the Gospel reading, in which God renews that promise by supplying bread in the form of the Son, Jesus.

The Letter to the Ephesians tells them to set aside their old ways of doing things and be new people created in Christ. It probably was much easier for the Ephesians to live as they were formerly accustomed to. Being Christ-minded is hard work. It means thinking in a new way and seeing everything with God's compassionate love.

In the Gospel reading, Jesus recognizes that the people are really excited about his miracle of giving them bread to eat. He tells them that they need more than just the bread that keeps their stomachs from growling. He wants them to understand that the real reason he multiplied the loaves and fishes—in last week's Gospel—is that he wants their faith to increase as well. He wants to satisfy a deeper human hunger for unity and oneness with the Bread of Life that lasts forever, himself.

When Jesus tells the people that God is sending bread for life eternal, they ask him to give them this bread always. They are not able to see that their living bread is Jesus, standing right in their midst.

Themes for Teens   The following themes from the Scriptures relate to the lives of teens:
- God hears us when we grumble.
- The Lord gives us bread to eat.
- Jesus is our bread from heaven.
- Jesus is the Bread of Life.
- Fill your emptiness with Christ.

Our Response

Activity   **Put on Christ**

This activity is keyed to the reading from Ephesians. It challenges the teens to find concrete ways to imitate Christ in their own life.

Form small groups. Direct each group to make a sandwich-board sign, using two pieces of poster board, a hole puncher, and string. Invite a volunteer from each group to stand in the center of the group and put on the sandwich-board sign, providing a blank writing space on the front and back of the sign.

Read Eph. 4:17,20–24 aloud and allow a few minutes for reflection. Then give each group a set of markers. Direct the teens to identify concrete ways they can imitate Christ or put on Christ. As answers are given, have a recorder in each group write them on its sandwich board. Tell each group to discuss the answers among themselves. When the small-group discussions are finished, invite the persons wearing the sandwich boards to display the answers on them to the whole group.

Activity Ideas   The following activity ideas also relate to the Scripture readings. You may want to read the passage(s) indicated as part of the activity.

- Instead of manna falling from the sky, how about questions falling from the ceiling? Draft some discussion questions based on today's readings. Write the questions on index cards and hang them from the ceiling all throughout your parish or school building. Send small groups of teens on a discussion question hunt. Whenever they find a question, the group should stop and answer it together before moving on to the next one. Here are some questions to get you started:
  ○ When have you grumbled at God for not getting what you want?
  ○ Do you believe in God only when your prayers are answered? Why?
  ○ How has God answered your prayers?

    (Exod. 16:2–4,12–15)

- Using a sacramentary, show the teens some different versions of the eucharistic prayers used during the liturgy. Discuss these different forms of prayer with them. (All readings)

- Direct the teens to create and present funny skits on ways God might answer prayers in our modern world, for example, by e-mail, fax, cellular phone, or CD-ROM. Allow the humor to lead into a witness or sharing on the ways God has answered some personal prayers. (Exod. 16:2–4,12–15)

- Offer the following questions for reflection and journal writing:
  ○ How does the bread of the Eucharist nourish you throughout the week?
  ○ When you pray "give us this day our daily bread," what are you asking for?

    (John 6:24–35)

- Lead a discussion on the deeper hungers we have and how the Eucharist can be nourishing bread for them. Also ask how we can be nourishing bread for the deeper hungers of others. (John 6:24–35)

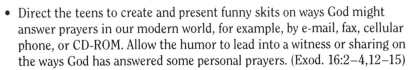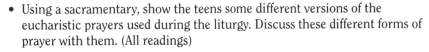

Ordinary Time

101

Nineteenth Sunday of the Year

Scripture Readings (117)
- ❖ 1 Kings 19:4–8
- ❖ Ps. 34:2–3,4–5,6–7,8–9
- ❖ Eph. 4:30—5:2
- ❖ John 6:41–51

God's Word

A major theme of the Scripture readings is "Food for the journey."

In the First Book of Kings, Elijah's life has become like a journey across the desert; it is so tough for him that he wishes he were dead. So, after a day's journey, he gives up and goes to sleep. An angel wakes him and tells him to eat the cake and drink the water that has appeared. This food from heaven nourishes him so well that he treks on for forty days and nights across the desert to God's mountain.

The psalmist calls us to use all our senses to taste and see the goodness of the Lord. This is a great lead-in to the continuing discourse on the bread of life found in the Gospel.

The Letter to the Ephesians relates a laundry list of things to get rid of—passion, anger, harsh words, slander, and malice—all things that do violence to the spirit that has been bestowed. We are asked to replace them with forgiveness and compassion, and, in doing so, to imitate Christ and become a prayer and offering to God.

The Gospel reading shows that miracles do not always guarantee faith. Even after the miracle of the loaves and fishes, the Jews had started to doubt and ask, "Wait a minute. Who is this guy?" The people could not get beyond appearances. For them, bread was bread. They could see Jesus only with physical eyes, instead of with the eyes of faith.

This is one of the few times the Gospels show Jesus talking clearly about his close relationship with the Father. He reaffirms his teaching that he is indeed the Bread of Life and speaks of the sacrifice he will make at the end of his journey here on earth—his flesh for the life of the world.

Themes for Teens

The following themes from the Scriptures relate to the lives of teens:
- Jesus is food for the journey.
- Wake up or you might miss your call.
- Experience the Lord.
- Imitate Christ.
- Jesus is our Living Bread.

Our Response

Activity Taste, See, Touch, Smell, Hear the Goodness of the Lord

This activity is keyed to the psalm. It invites the teens to use their senses to become more alert to the many ways God touches their life every day.

Give the teens each a copy of Ps. 34:2–3,4–5,6–7,8–9. Ask them to read the psalm right after they wake up the next morning and to write each of the five senses—hearing, taste, sight, smell, and touch—on a separate page in a small notebook. Tell them that as they go through their day, they should jot down ways they observe God's presence in the world around them, noting the observation under the appropriate sense. Direct them to read the psalm again before they go to sleep that night.

Invite them to bring along their notebook and share their discoveries the next time you meet as a group. Lead a discussion on recognizing the many ways God provides bread for our deeper hungers.

Activity Ideas

The following activity ideas also relate to the Scripture readings. You may want to read the passage(s) indicated as part of the activity.

- Simulate Elijah's journey across the desert to the mountain of the Lord. Even if there are no deserts or mountains nearby, pack a lunch and go on a group hike to a designated destination. Stop along the way to be nourished by food and by the Word. At each stop, eat part of your lunch. Then read and discuss one of the three readings or the psalm. (All readings)

- Ask the teens to plan an activity hour for children in your parish called "Walk in the Footsteps of Christ." The teens can lead the children in games such as Follow Christ (played like Follow the Leader) and Jesus Says (played like Simon Says). (Eph. 4:30—5:2)

- Inquire how your parish prepares people to serve as eucharistic ministers. Invite a eucharistic minister to come and share with the teens her or his reason for becoming one and how it has deepened her or his relationship with Jesus and with others. (John 6:41–51)

- Form the teens into pairs. Ask them to stand, face each other, and remain silent during this activity. Direct one of the partners to mime one way Christ related with people. The other partner should silently mirror the action. Then tell the partners to reverse roles and repeat the activity. (Eph. 4:30—5:2)

Twentieth Sunday of the Year

Scripture Readings (120)

❖ Prov. 9:1–6
❖ Ps. 34:2–3,10–11,12–13,14–15
❖ Eph. 5:15–20
❖ John 6:51–58

God's Word

A major theme of the Scripture readings is "Making wise choices."

These readings communicate that the choices we make in life are often difficult. In the reading from Proverbs, Wisdom sends out an invitation to feast at her table of nourishing food. But to respond to the invitation means making a choice—a choice between foolishness and wisdom. Which is more attractive? In this reading, wisdom is quite appealing, but often in our life, foolishness appears more attractive.

Ordinary Time

As in last Sunday's psalm, we hear the psalmist urging people to experience the wonders of the Lord. This time, however, the message is for the poor and the lowly—not the great—and for those who turn away from evil.

Echoing the first reading, the writer of the Letter to the Ephesians tells the people not to act like fools in order to guard against evil ways. He wants them to trade in getting drunk for singing psalms. It may sound like the psalmist wants us to spend all our time in church, but, in fact, the call is to make the right choices. Jesus' words in the Gospel reading are really tough for the crowds to swallow. They aren't cannibals, and all this talk about eating flesh and drinking blood makes them nervous.

Jesus' words, understood for their deeper meaning, reflect the Catholic conviction that the bread and wine shared by the parish community in the Eucharist are the real body and blood of Christ. And when the bread and wine are taken, the parish community is nourished, strengthened, and bonded together more deeply together in the Lord. Those who participate in the Eucharist become one with the Lord, both as individuals and as a community.

Themes for Teens

The following themes from the Scriptures relate to the lives of teens:
- Don't be a fool; wise up.
- Wise up; follow Christ.
- Turn away from the foolishness of evil.
- Attend Mass; become one with Christ.
- Jesus feeds us with his body and blood.

Our Response

Activity   Evil Inside and Out

 This activity is keyed to the first three readings. It is a craft project that helps the teens recognize that things are not always as they appear. Often evil and foolishness can be wrapped in attractive and enticing packages.

Direct each teen to bring two magazines to the next group meeting. Provide scissors and glue. Say something like the following:

> These readings today tell us to watch out for evil in our life. But that isn't always easy. Do you know evil when you see it? Does it sometimes wear a disguise? For example, advertising can portray consumerism and personal wealth as very attractive, thus urging you to buy more and more things. Yet consumerism and materialism that put things before people are evil. Also, music videos and movies portray sex as exciting and something you must do now if you are to fit in, when, in fact, such activity can destroy relationships and self-worth. Can you think of any more examples?

Give each teen a large white envelope. On the outside of the envelope, instruct them to glue pictures or words of attractive things that entice us to foolish and even sinful ways. Direct them to glue, on a separate sheet of paper, pictures or words that show what evil really lurks behind those false appearances. Tell them to stuff this sheet into the envelope.

Close by reading Eph. 5:15–20 together and then offering a brief prayer asking God's guidance to help us look beyond appearances and make the right choices to avoid evil in our life.

Activity Ideas   The following activity ideas also relate to the Scripture readings. You may want to read the passage(s) indicated as part of the activity.

- Include as part of a youth group lock-in a 40-hour devotion to Jesus present in the Blessed Sacrament. Encourage each teen to sign up to stay with Jesus and pray with him in his sacramental presence for half an hour. Suggest that the teens use this time to reflect on the prayer said during the liturgy of the Eucharist: "Lord, I am not worthy to receive you, but only say the word and I shall be healed." (John 6:51–58)

- Direct the teens to think about all the things they enjoy at a party or celebration with their friends, for example, the invitations, the decorations, the food. Ask them to compare these celebrations with our celebration of the Eucharist as a community. What do the celebrations have in common? As a service project, instruct the teens to send Mass invitations to other teens who do not attend regularly. (John 6:51–58)

- Ask the teens to name the seven gifts of the Holy Spirit (wisdom, understanding, knowledge, courage, right judgment, reverence, and wonder and awe.) Then read Eph. 5:15–20 aloud and ask which of these gifts is highlighted in the reading. Stress that the Spirit gives these gifts to help guide us in making choices in our life. Divide the teens into seven groups. Assign each group one of the seven gifts. Direct them to come up with one real-life situation in which use of this gift will help them make the right choice. (Prov. 9:1–6; Ps. 34:2–3,10–11,12–13,14–15; Eph. 5:15–20)

- After reflecting on the Bread of Life readings from the past three weeks, consider having your class or youth group prepare and celebrate the liturgy together. (John 6:51–58)

Twenty-first Sunday of the Year

Scripture Readings (123)
- ❖ Josh. 24:1–2,15–17,18
- ❖ Ps. 34:2–3,16–17,18–19,20–21,22–23
- ❖ Eph. 5:21–32
- ❖ John 6:60–69

God's Word   A major theme of the Scripture readings is "The challenge of faith."

In the first reading, Joshua gathers all the people together and asks, "What do you stand for? Who do you stand for?" The people stop to recall all the miracles, the salvation, and the compassion God has bestowed on them. They reach the conclusion that the proper response to God's loving service to them is to be of service to God. Joshua actually pledges his whole household to serve the Lord.

The psalm refrain is familiar and comfortable after appearing for three Sundays, but these particular verses highlight God as protector, as a shield against all the evil we might encounter. The psalmist's confidence in the Lord's special care for those broken in body or spirit is especially encouraging.

Ordinary Time

The reading from the Letter to the Ephesians was written in a patriarchal culture. In a modern perspective, it seems to support gender inequality. However, it actually reflects a substantial advance toward gender equality. The writer compares God's love for the church with the love of two people in a marriage and, in doing so, celebrates the sacredness of the marriage relationship. The last part of the reading forms the basis for our understanding of marriage as a sacrament.

The Gospel reading portrays many of Jesus' disciples having their faith shaken. Some leave Jesus behind. The responsibilities of being loyal to him are getting more real and demanding. And the startling revelation that union with Jesus is to be by way of bread made flesh and wine made blood is just too tough to take. Yet the Apostles remain steadfast. Peter's profession of faith expresses the need for a quantum leap of faith in Christ.

We are not unlike the Apostles. Our faith in Christ is challenged by those around us. Our faith makes demands that often involve risking something of ourselves to continue to follow him.

Themes for Teens

The following themes from the Scriptures relate to the lives of teens:
- Who do you stand for?
- God heals the brokenhearted.
- God loves the church deeply.
- You have reached a crossroads in your faith.
- Jesus' message is tough to swallow.

Our Response

Activity

We Will Serve the Lord

This activity is keyed to the first reading. It helps the teens understand their vital role in the wider community, elevates their self-worth, and recognizes that they make a difference in both small and large ways.

Read Josh. 24:1–2,15–17,18 together and allow a few minutes for silent reflection.

Next, on a long strip of computer paper, write in large block letters the phrase, "As for us and our group, we will serve the Lord." Invite everyone to take a marker and sign their name on the banner. Then have them think about three things they do or could do to serve the Lord's work. If they get stuck, ask them to think of things they could do to help others or give praise to God in the following settings: home, school, and parish.

Using markers of different colors than the ones used previously, invite the teens to write on the banner three ways they can serve the Lord. Because this is a time of year when a youth group or class is likely planning its fall calendar, ask the teens to consider making a pledge to carry out some of the suggestions on the banner as service projects during the fall. If possible, hang this pledge in your meeting space.

Activity Ideas

The following activity ideas also relate to the Scripture readings. You may want to read the passage(s) indicated as part of the activity.

- Give the young people time to write in their journal an answer to the question, How would you respond if Jesus asked you the same question he put to the Apostles: "'Do you want to leave me too?'" (John 6:60–69)

- Invite the teens to describe situations in which they have been put down for what they believe. Ask them how our society in general puts down faith in Christ and his message? Direct them to think about the kind of courage the faithful Apostles had to have to remain loyal to Jesus. Compare the courage of the Apostles with the kind of courage needed in today's world to stand up for what you believe. (John 6:60–69)

- Make a giant shield out of poster board and put it in the center of the prayer space. After reading today's psalm, invite the teens to come up one at a time and write a prayer thanking God for protection or asking God to protect them or a family member from evil. (Ps. 34:2–3,16–17,18–19,20–21,22–23)

- Urge the teens to read the first reading at home with their family and to reflect together on ways their family does or could serve the Lord. Later, collect a list of things the teens did with their family and publish it in the parish bulletin or newsletter as examples of family service projects. (Josh. 24:1–2,15–17,18)

Twenty-second Sunday of the Year

Scripture Readings (126)

- ❖ Deut. 4:1–2,6–8
- ❖ Ps. 15:2–3,3–4,4–5
- ❖ James 1:17–18,21–22,27
- ❖ Mark 7:1–8,14–15,21–23

God's Word

A major theme of the Scripture readings is "Keeping God's laws."

In the first reading, Moses calls on the people to do more than just hear the commands of God. He challenges them to live them. Adding or subtracting from what God has told them to do is not up to them. In living carefully the laws and statutes of their God, the Israelites will not only impress other nations with their wisdom and intelligence but will become examples for other nations to follow. They will reveal to the nations a God who is close to them and present in their need.

The responsorial psalm tells us that God is just, and God requires justice from us. Justice is done with words and actions that are rooted in and carried in one's heart. A just person does not harm others, either with hands or words.

The Letter of James echoes the first reading with a call to be doers of the Word, rather than just listeners. We are called to be thankful for the gift of God's word, allowing it to take root and grow in us. We are asked not to hide from the world in fear of evil, but to walk in the world living God's word, looking after poor and hurting people, and avoiding the stain of sin.

In the Gospel reading, the Pharisees get hung up on the details of the law instead of following the spirit of the law. Their power to enforce human traditions, often at the expense of the poor and needy, becomes more important than following God's law, which looks to the poor and needy. Jesus rebukes them saying, in effect, that God's favor for the poor and needy is more important than the enforcement of the details of their laws.

Human traditions can never take priority over the laws of God. Jesus is not telling the Pharisees to get rid of their laws, but to rethink their priorities.

Ordinary Time

God is honored more by heartfelt actions toward others than by obeying laws or performing rituals that are insensitive to poor and needy people.

Themes for Teens

The following themes from the Scriptures relate to the lives of teens:
- Wisdom is found in the commandments of God.
- The just person walks with God.
- All gifts come from God.
- Live the word of God.
- When in conflict, follow the laws of God, not human laws.

Our Response

Activity

Whose Law Is It Anyway?

This activity is keyed to the Gospel reading. Before your next meeting or class, ask each teen to bring an example of a law recently passed by Congress, the state legislature, or the local government.

In small groups, direct each teen to describe the law he or she discovered. Ask whether this civil law respects the commandments of God. For example, federal law guarantees the right to an abortion, yet this goes against the law of God to protect all forms of human life.

Discuss the role lobbyists play in trying to get laws passed. Many represent big money and big business. Challenge the teens to be a voice in making sure the laws of our land match the spirit of God's law, which looks first to poor and needy people. Ask how we as Christians can make sure our legal system advocates for poor and needy people.

Give the teens a list of the names and addresses of their representatives in government. Urge them to pick an issue and write a letter expressing their view on it. Encourage them to be a watchdog and a voice in the legislative process of creating laws in our society.

Activity Ideas

The following activity ideas also relate to the Scripture readings. You may want to read the passage(s) indicated as part of the activity.

- Send the teens to the Scriptures to find other examples of the way Jesus lived a just life, especially in the way he advocated for poor and marginalized people. Challenge the teens to find parallels in their own life and experiences. (Mark 7:1–8,14–15,21–23)

- Start a discussion with this statement: That which is right is not always easy. Give the teens some examples of tough choices. Ask them what choices they would make in those situations. Try to obtain a copy of the game Scruples, from Milton Bradley, and play this life-choice game with your group. (Ps. 15:2–3,3–4,4–5; James 1:17–18,21–22,27)

- Sing the psalm refrain, and instead of using the Scripture verses, offer contemporary examples of people and groups who live what they believe despite the cost. Some examples are people who fight for drug-free or gun-free zones around schools, Mothers Against Drunk Driving (MADD), and Neighborhood Watch programs. (Ps. 15:2–3,3–4,4–5)

- Put up a world map. Each time you gather as a group, note an injustice taking place in a country or different part of the world and pray for the need of God's kind of justice there. (Ps. 15:2–3,3–4,4–5; James 1:17–18,21–22,27)

Twenty-third Sunday of the Year

Scripture Readings (129)

- ❖ Isa. 35:4–7
- ❖ Ps. 146:7,8–9,9–10
- ❖ James 2:1–5
- ❖ Mark 7:31–37

God's Word

A major theme of the Scripture readings is "Open your eyes to God in your life."

Isaiah tells of the God who works wonders and miracles. In adversity, God is there to give strength in the face of fear. There is nothing God cannot do with regard to human nature or the powers of nature. God heals our deafness and blindness, and makes the dry land burst with water. God is a God of powerful change in our world and in our life.

The responsorial psalm praises God for the many wonders God has worked. God is praised for being just and kind, for lifting up the oppressed, the hungry, the captives. Those who have the least—strangers, homeless people, or orphans—God places first. The Lord cares deeply for those in greatest need.

In the Letter of James, we are admonished not to be misled by outside appearances. What is inside is what really counts in the end. Wealthy and well-dressed people are not to be held in more esteem than poor people. Rather, poor people in the eyes of the world are often rich with faith and are the heirs to the Kingdom promised by God.

In the Gospel reading, Jesus restores the gifts of hearing and speech to a man who was both deaf and mute. Thus, Jesus fulfills the promise of the first reading—when the deaf hear and the blind see, God is present. The miracles reveal a God who frees us from the darkness and silence of sin. The miracles also open our eyes to God's wonders and give us a voice to proclaim God's word.

Themes for Teens

The following themes from the Scriptures relate to the lives of teens:
- God opens our eyes and ears.
- The Lord champions the poor.
- What is inside counts the most.
- God frees us from the darkness and silence of sin.
- We need to be open to God.

Our Response

Activity

Open Your Eyes, Open Your Ears

This activity is keyed to the Gospel reading. It encourages the teens to look and hear attentively. Give each person a set of earplugs or two cotton balls. Ask them to put them in their ears so that they are unable to hear anything. Another alternative would be for you to stand on the other side of a large window where the teens can see you but cannot hear you.

When no one is able to hear you, read aloud today's Gospel reading. When you are finished, ask the teens to take out their earplugs and tell you what the Gospel was about. When they are unable to tell you, pose the question, What are some of the things that make us deaf to the word of God? Are there times when you hear the Gospel being proclaimed but you aren't really listening?

Give each teen a Bible and a blindfold. Direct the teens to put on their blindfold and make sure they cannot see at all. Tell them not to remove their blindfold until they are told to do so. Ask them to turn to the specific page where today's Gospel reading is found. Allow time for them to read it. When they are unable to do so, ask the question, What are some of the things that make us blind to the word of God? Are there times when you have read from the Bible but weren't really able to understand it?

Allow the teens to take off their blindfold. Talk about how we need to spend time with God and pay attention to God's word around us. Stress the need for quiet in order to hear God. In silence, we can listen and hear God better, and we can speak more clearly in return.

Give the teens plenty of room to spread out and create their own quiet space. Insist on silence during this time. Ask the teens to spend 20 minutes reading today's Gospel passage and answering the question, How can we move from spiritual deafness to really listening to the word of God? How can we move from spiritual blindness to seeing the word of God all around us?

Activity Ideas

The following activity ideas also relate to the Scripture readings. You may want to read the passage(s) indicated as part of the activity.

- Teach the young people the song "Cry of the Poor," by John Foley (*Glory and Praise,* vol. 2, no. 93). Ask the question, How does God hear the cry of the poor? Talk about how God answers the cry of the poor through us. Challenge the teens to do a better job of listening to this cry and doing something about it. Affirm the importance of every individual contribution. (Isa. 35:4–7; Ps. 146:7,8–9,9–10; James 2:1–5)

- Invite a vowed religious to talk about the vow of poverty. How does he or she live out that vow? How does he or she live a simple life? Ask the teens to examine one week of their life and list some strategies for living more simply. (James 2:1–5)

- Direct the teens to read today's Gospel account and talk about the signs and rituals Jesus used in healing the deaf and mute man. Share with them the ritual involved in the sacrament of anointing. Encourage them to point out similarities and differences between these rituals. Use this discussion as an opportunity to help the teens understand an often misunderstood sacrament. (Mark 7:31–37)

- Ask the teens to list the three most valuable or expensive things they own. Have them itemize how they spent their money in the last month and mark with an *A* money spent on items that are essential, with a *B* money spent on luxuries, and with a *C* money spent on items that are for other people. Lead a discussion of the following questions:
  ○ Can someone be poor in material things and rich in faith?
  ○ Can someone be rich in material things and poor in faith?
  ○ What does it mean to be rich in faith?

(James 2:1–5)

Twenty-fourth Sunday of the Year

Scripture Readings (132)

- ❖ Isa. 50:4–9
- ❖ Ps. 116:1–2,3–4,5–6,8–9
- ❖ James 2:14–18
- ❖ Mark 8:27–35

God's Word

A major theme of the Scripture readings is "Who do you say that I am?"

In the first reading, the prophet is comforted by God, who stands beside him in the face of all adversity. The prophet is faithful in proclaiming God's compassion regardless of the abuse he receives in return. This reading foreshadows the suffering Jesus endured before his death. Even though God is on our side, we know we must often suffer in order to do what is right.

The psalm speaks of a God who is close, a God who walks with us on earth, in the land of the living. Especially hopeful is the verse "For [God] has freed my soul from death, / my eyes from tears, my feet from stumbling." Suffering will have an end in God. We speak of a God who helps us walk on the right paths, comforts us when we feel sad, and protects us from the violence and killing in our society.

The Letter of James makes it clear that the God revealed in Jesus is a God who sees faith and good works as absolutely connected. Living the faith is not an option for disciples of Jesus. Living one's faith deepens that faith. Is it possible to read this passage and not hear God asking us to clothe the homeless and feed the hungry?

In the Gospel reading, Jesus asks his disciples who they and others think he is. They voice what they want him to be—a messiah, a savior. Jesus acknowledges that role but tells them that carrying it out will involve suffering and being put to death. This is hard for the disciples to accept. But Jesus is firm, pointing out that this is also true for anyone who chooses to follow him.

What a tough choice: If you try to save your life by looking out only for yourself, you will lose it. If you lose your life in service to others, you will save it. The price of following the Gospel often has the appearance, even the experience, of losing something of oneself and one's possessions. But the return is life on a deeper level that endures forever.

Themes for Teens

The following themes from the Scriptures relate to the lives of teens:
- God is my help.
- I will walk with God.
- Faith and action go hand in hand.
- "You are the Messiah."
- Following the Gospel often includes losing something of one's self.

Our Response

Activity

Three Prayers in One

This activity is keyed to the Gospel reading. First, spend some time giving the teens an overview of different forms of prayer: quiet prayer, storytelling, scriptural prayer, creative prayer, prayer in different settings, drama, dance, mime, traditional prayer, shared prayer, musical prayer, symbols and prayer, high-tech prayer, and so forth.

Then divide them into three groups and tell them that each group will be planning part of a prayer service. Each part is to take only 5 minutes, for a total prayer service time of 15 minutes. Ask them to use no more than two forms of prayer for their segment.

Share the Gospel reading with the group. Repeat the verse: "'If a man wishes to come after me, he must deny his very self, take up his cross, and follow in my steps.'"

Assign the parts of the prayer service as follows:

- *Group 1.* Deny yourself.
- *Group 2.* Take up your cross.
- *Group 3.* Follow in Jesus' steps.

Direct the small groups to reflect on the meaning of their part of the Gospel and then write a prayer for their portion of the prayer service. Touch base during the planning time to answer any questions. Encourage prayerful reflection on the words of Jesus, and stress the importance of using a variety of prayer forms to communicate with God.

When the groups are ready, knit the pieces together into one prayer service that can be shared later in your meeting or at the next meeting.

For more information on different forms of prayer to use with youth, see *Pathways to Praying with Teens,* by Maryann Hakowski (Winona, MN: Saint Mary's Press, 1993).

Activity Ideas

The following activity ideas also relate to the Scripture readings. You may want to read the passage(s) indicated as part of the activity.

- Do we live what we believe? Give each teen a copy of the creed we proclaim every Sunday at the liturgy. Take it line by line or section by section and discuss ways we can put that faith into action. Later, give the teens some time alone to choose one part of the creed and pray about how they hope to live what they believe more closely. (James 2:14–18)

- How would you live your life differently if Jesus were walking by your side? Show the movie *O God,* starring John Denver and George Burns. Afterward, divide the teens into small groups to plan skits. Direct them to choose a scene from school or home and act out what would happen if God showed up one day. (Isa. 50:4–9)

- Lead the guided meditation "Who do you say that I am?" by Thomas F. Catucci, in *Time with Jesus: Twenty Guided Meditations for Youth* (Notre Dame, IN: Ave Maria Press, 1993), pages 99–104. After the meditation, ask the teens to reflect on this question in their journal: If Jesus turned to you and said, "'Who do you say that I am?'" what would you say? (Mark 8:27–35)

- Ask the teens to explore what your parish or school is already doing to feed the hungry or take care of the homeless. Challenge them to plan and organize an ongoing outreach project for needy people—not a once-and-done event—or to work in an outreach effort already in operation, such as a homeless shelter or a soup kitchen. Challenge them to take part in service efforts that provide real contact between themselves and the people they are serving. (Ps. 116:1–2,3–4,5–6,8–9; James 2:14–18)

Twenty-fifth Sunday of the Year

Scripture Readings (135)

❖ Wis. 2:12,17–20
❖ Ps. 54:3–4,5,6–8
❖ James 3:16—4:3
❖ Mark 9:30–37

God's Word

A major theme of the Scripture readings is "The risks of serving God."

According to the Book of Wisdom, it would be a lot easier to keep quiet than to stand up for what one believes. Wicked people are all waiting to challenge, test, and trap the upright person. The wicked just can't stand the wise.

The psalm refrain, "The Lord upholds my life," is an image of God as the preserver of life of those who in following the way of God's call are vulnerable to suffering at the hands of the wicked.

The Letter of James reminds us that our task is to be peacemakers. But the task is not an easy one—it makes us vulnerable. James points out that the seeds of conflict and war are greed and jealousy, and that we can only harvest peace if we plant the seeds of peace. War—no matter where it is fought—begins in the heart. There, too, is where peace must take root.

In the Gospel reading, Jesus feels terribly frustrated. He is trying to share with the disciples the agony of his anticipated death and, at the same time, his hope in resurrection. All this time, the disciples are busy arguing among themselves over who is the most important. They do not understand that to be a leader in Jesus' mission one must first be a servant, even though doing so may involve suffering. Following Jesus means changing priorities—seeking not power or fame, but welcoming the weak and the lowly, those who have no more power than a child. When we welcome the outcast or the needy, we welcome Jesus and we welcome God, the Father.

Themes for Teens

The following themes from the Scriptures relate to the lives of teens:

- God will take care of us.
- The Lord lifts up my life.
- Sow the seeds of peace.
- Be a servant first.
- Welcome the children.

Our Response

Activity

Servants Behind the Scenes

This activity is keyed to the readings as a whole. Your school or parish includes people who are dedicated to serving others. Many of them do not get any recognition and do not seek it out, yet their gifts to the community and individuals are invaluable.

Choose a week when you can honor these people. Direct the teens to identify them and brainstorm ways they can highlight their service. Here are some ideas:

- Take pictures of the parish teachers and put them on a bulletin board of honor.
- Profile the good works of a teacher each month in the student newspaper.
- Give a bouquet of flowers to the parish secretary, who finds time to type your youth group newsletter.
- Say thank you to the lectors who proclaim the Scriptures every week.
- Give the parish lawn-care crew a break by taking over their duties for one week.
- Track down the school custodian and treat her or him to an ice cream cone one day.

Don't forget to honor the children and youth who take part in service efforts.

Stress that we are *all* called to service by our baptism as Catholic Christians. Encourage the young people who have not yet participated in service to match their gifts and talents with the needs of the community.

Activity Ideas

The following activity ideas also relate to the Scripture readings. You may want to read the passage(s) indicated as part of the activity.

- Read the first Scripture passage aloud and then encourage the teens to tell stories of times they were challenged because of what they believe. How did they react? Lead a discussion of these questions:
  - ○ Why is peer pressure so strong?
  - ○ Why is it hard to risk standing up for what one believes?
  - ○ What are we afraid of?

(Wis. 2:12,17–20)

- Show the video *One in a Million* (Mars Hill Productions) about a young man who envisions what life would be like if he had never lived. Lead a discussion on how the psalm, when combined with this video, challenges us to stand up for values we personally hold dear in our life. See the list of audio-visual distributors on page 133 for more information. (Ps. 54:3–4,5,6–8)

- Direct the teens to reflect on the second reading and think of a conflict they are facing right now. What are the causes? How did it start?

  Ask them how they can sow seeds of peace. Note that seeds are small and that the beginning of peace often starts small—with someone willing to take the first step or make the first move. Tell them to consider sending a packet of seeds to someone with a copy of this reading and a note of apology, if appropriate. (James 3:16—4:3)

- The last line of the Gospel reads, "'Whoever welcomes me welcomes, not me, but [the One] who sent me.'" Ask the young people to reflect on the last twenty-four hours and write answers to these questions in their journal:
  - ○ When did you welcome Jesus and God, the Father?
  - ○ When did you miss an opportunity to welcome them?

(Mark 9:30–37)

Twenty-sixth Sunday of the Year

Scripture Readings (138)

- ❖ Num. 11:25–29
- ❖ Ps. 19:8,10,12–13,14
- ❖ James 5:1–6
- ❖ Mark 9:38–43,45,47–48

God's Word

A major theme of the Scripture readings is "God's way versus our way."

In the reading from Numbers, the spirit bestowed on Moses is shared with the elders so that Moses is no longer the only one who can prophesy. Two of the elders who are not present when the spirit is shared, nevertheless began to prophesy. A young man expects Moses to respond with jealousy when this takes place. Instead Moses welcomes the sharing of the gift and explains that he wishes all people could be prophets and experience the Lord's Spirit.

The psalm joyfully praises God as the Just Judge, who wisely sets laws for the people to follow. The psalmist seeks to serve the Lord by following God's rules. This response may seem odd because precepts and law are not something we connect with joy. Sometimes following the rules seems like nothing more than a burden. Could it be that our notion and purpose of law is quite different from that of God's?

The reading from the Letter of James is aimed at those whose main goal in life is getting rich. Many people get rich from exploiting others. We see it in our own country and around the world. If we are busy collecting and possessing wealth, we don't have much room for people in our life.

In the Gospel reading, the disciples, like some of the people in the first reading, are jealous of the gifts of others. They complain about someone else healing in God's name. Like Moses, Jesus welcomes the good being done by those outside their group and sees it as being joined with the good done by the community of disciples. On the other hand, evildoers should not be tolerated, and if they are members of the community, they should be cut off much like a body part whose disease threatens the health of the whole body.

Themes for Teens

The following themes from the Scriptures relate to the lives of teens:
- Don't be jealous of others' gifts.
- Share the Spirit.
- Following Jesus can bring us joy.
- Wealth can devour you.
- Don't let possessiveness weigh you down.

Our Response

Activity

The Fork in the Road

This activity is keyed to the readings as a whole. On a large piece of butcher paper, draw an outline of a single road that splits into two distinct roads. Label one "God's Way" and the other "Our Way."

Introduce the activity in the following way:

In today's Scripture readings we face a contrast between the will of God and our own choices. Let's take a closer look at each reading and list what we find in each case.

Read one passage at a time and invite the teens to write their responses with marker on the butcher paper. It is likely to look something like this:

	God's Way	Our Way
First reading	Sharing the Spirit	Jealousy over gifts
Psalm	Joy in following the law	Slipping into wanton sin
Second reading	Doing what is right and just	Hoarding our wealth Cheating others out of a just wage
	Putting people before things	Putting possessions before people
Gospel reading	Allowing works in God's name	Restricting ministry work
	Ridding ourselves of causes of sin	Allowing our faults to lead us into sin

After this part of the exercise, divide the teens into small groups. Give each group a pad of Post-it notes and some pencils. Place an orange traffic cone in the center of each group.

Introduce this part of the session in words similar to the following:

What we just did is the first step in learning to walk in God's way rather than our own way—recognizing where we need to be. Yet we still face obstacles or barriers. In your group, discuss some of the barriers to our having a healthy relationship with God and others. In other words, what kinds of people, things, and circumstances can lead us to sin?

Rather than tear something out as the Gospel says, we'll settle for writing the examples on Post-it notes and putting them on our traffic cone. As you name a barrier, ask your group for suggestions on how to get around it or completely remove it from your road.

Activity Ideas The following activity ideas also relate to the Scripture readings. You may want to read the passage(s) indicated as part of the activity.

- Catch your group unaware by coming into your meeting with a bullhorn to get their attention. Direct a teen to read the Gospel passage and pose these questions:
  - How is this reading a wake-up call for us?
  - Why does God want to get our attention about the destructive nature of the sins of greed and possessiveness?

(Mark 9:38–43,45,47–48)

- Borrow a big rope and have a tug-of-war contest at the start of your meeting. Pose these questions:
  - What pulls us toward God?
  - What pulls us away from God?
  - What do the Scriptures tell us we need to get rid of so we aren't pulled away from God?

(Mark 9:38–43,45,47–48)

- Tell each teen to write down the career or type of job they would like to have once they are out of school. On the same piece of paper, direct them to list at least five specific reasons for pursuing this job. Ask them where "make a lot of money" fell on their list. Ask them where "serving others" fell on their list. In light of the second reading, encourage them to consider whether they should change their priorities. (James 5:1–6)

- If the teens still have a lot of trouble understanding the metaphor used in the Gospel reading, here's another one to share: If you have a plant on which the bottom leaves are getting a blight that threatens to kill the whole plant, would you leave it as such and allow the plant to die? No, you would likely remove the blighted leaves and put a fungicide on the plant to make sure the blight is eradicated. (Mark 9:38–43,45,47–48)

Twenty-seventh Sunday of the Year

Scripture Readings (141)
- ❖ Gen. 2:18–24
- ❖ Ps. 128:1–2,3,4–5,6
- ❖ Heb. 2:9–11
- ❖ Mark 10:2–16

God's Word

A major theme of the Scripture readings is "A covenant of love."

The reading from Genesis is part of the account of God making the world. God creates all sorts of animals and birds, but none are suitable partners for the human God has created. In the story we see that God creates the female from the same substance as the male. The Scriptures tell us that the man and the woman, as partners, are mutually interdependent. In a later, Christian perspective, the relationship between them is to be like God's relationship with humans—a covenant of love.

The psalm is a beautiful blessing expressing trust that God will keep God's part of the covenant. The psalm outlines, according to the standards of that day, all the good things that will happen if we are faithful to the Lord: we will have food to eat, a big family, prosperity, and a long life.

The reading from the Letter to the Hebrews talks about how far God will go to maintain the covenant—as far as to send Jesus as one of us and allow him to suffer and die for the sake of all of us. Because Jesus became one of us, we can share in his exultation.

Today's Gospel passage is often read at weddings. It is one of the few times in the Scriptures that Jesus talks about marriage. The Pharisees want to trap Jesus, so they decide to quiz him on issues of divorce, which their law allowed. Jesus puts a new perspective on that law—a perspective that restores woman as a partner with man in marriage, and restores marriage to its status as a sacred covenant. Jesus speaks of marriage as a union joined by God, which no person is to dissolve. It is a covenant between God and two people.

In the long form of this Gospel reading, Jesus also talks about the importance of making time for children. He holds them up as models for accepting the Kingdom of God. Children are to be welcomed and celebrated in the Christian community.

These readings celebrate a covenant between God and creation, a covenant shared with us through Jesus and a covenant of love between a husband and a wife that is passed on to their children in the Christian community.

Themes for Teens

The following themes from the Scriptures relate to the lives of teens:
- May the Lord bless you always.
- Jesus is our brother.
- Marriage is sacred.
- The two became one.
- Make time for children.

Our Response

Activity

A Wedding to Plan

This activity is keyed to the Gospel reading. Divide the teens into groups of eight. Ask a boy and a girl in each group to volunteer to be the "bride and groom" for this exercise. Tell the teens they have just become wedding planners for the couple in their group. Give them 30 minutes to help their couple prepare for their wedding. Do not give them specific instructions, but ask them to provide as much detail as possible.

When they are finished, invite each group to present the wedding plans for its bride and groom. Make a point of noticing how much of the plans center around the superficial—wedding cake, photographer, color of tuxedos—and how much center around the spiritual aspects of the wedding—picking the right Scripture readings, discussing how God will fit into their marriage, and the like.

Pass a small paper honeycomb wedding bell around each group. The person holding the bell is the one who can speak during discussion of the following questions:
- Do most couples spend more time worrying about the fleeting parts of preparing for a wedding instead of the more lasting issues?
- What types of issues should a couple talk about before they get married?
- How can faith and spirituality have a role in a wedding celebration?
- How can a couple include God and faith in their marriage?
- What is the difference between a civil marriage and the sacrament of marriage?
- What makes a marriage a sacrament?

Read aloud Mark 10:2–16. Then ask the group what Jesus is trying to teach us about the covenant of marriage.

Activity Ideas

The following activity ideas also relate to the Scripture readings. You may want to read the passage(s) indicated as part of the activity.

- Divide the teens into small groups. Direct them to read the psalm together and then to write updated verses that include people and things that are blessings in their life. Invite the teens to share their updated psalms during prayer together. (Ps. 128:1–2,3,4–5,6)

- Invite one or two couples who are active in the Marriage Encounter or Engaged Encounter movement to share their reflections on the role of God and faith in their marriage. Consider inviting both a couple that has been married a few years and a couple that has been married for a long time. (Gen. 2:18–24; Mark 10:2–16)

- Divide the teens into two teams and debate both sides of these two approaches to marriage:
  - "It's better to live together before getting married."
  - "Well, if it doesn't work out, I can always get a divorce."
    Then read aloud today's Gospel passage and talk about how Jesus might respond to each of these statements. End by sharing some of the church's teaching on these subjects. (Mark 10:2–16)

- Watch the movie *Father of the Bride,* starring Steve Martin. Afterward, direct the teens to write down as many details as they can of the wedding planning. Ask them what percentage of the movie dealt with the spiritual aspect of marriage. (All readings)

Twenty-eighth Sunday of the Year

Scripture Readings (144)

- ❖ Wis. 7:7–11
- ❖ Ps. 90:12–13,14–15,16–17
- ❖ Heb. 4:12–13
- ❖ Mark 10:17–30

God's Word

A major theme of the Scripture readings is "The cost of discipleship."

The first reading compares and contrasts the gift of wisdom with the desire for riches and power. Wisdom wins by a mile. Wisdom is the gift of knowing that possessing riches and power is not the greatest value, nor a lasting one. To which do we give the higher value in our life—riches or wisdom?

The psalmist believes wisdom is to know that joy comes from God's tremendous love and asks for wisdom of heart that keeps this knowledge firm. The psalmist also knows that there is a price to be paid to gain wisdom—that it is gained from both good times and bad.

Like the psalmist, the author of the Letter to the Hebrews recognizes the power of God's word. Like a two-edged sword, it cuts to the depths of our being, revealing to us both God and ourselves.

The Gospel story presents a young man seeking wisdom. He asks Jesus the question, "'Good Teacher, what must I do to share in everlasting life?'" First, Jesus reminds him to follow the Commandments, which he was already doing. But then Jesus asks the young man to give away all his possessions and follow him.

Ordinary Time

The young man's reaction shows the difficulty the early Christian community faced in following the call to discipleship—a call that meant becoming possession-poor. They must have started to think that salvation was impossible. But their faith in the power of God in Jesus is reflected in the account, as Jesus looks at the young man with love and promises that with God all is possible.

The camel's eye analogy shows us how truly radical following Jesus can be. Just obeying the Commandments isn't enough. As a Christian community, we need to reach out and share what we have. And in living that way, all things are possible with God.

Themes for Teens

The following themes from the Scriptures relate to the lives of teens:
- Wisdom is worth more than wealth.
- Take joy in God's love.
- God's word reveals all.
- Discipleship can be costly.
- All things are possible with God.

Our Response

Activity

Disciples Wanted

This activity is keyed to the Gospel reading. Direct the teens to look through the Christian Testament for some of Jesus' other teachings on how to be a disciple, noting both the passages cited and the teachings described in them.

Next, invite the teens to write a job description for a modern disciple. They can write it in the form of a help-wanted ad that someone would place in the classifieds or post on an Internet bulletin board.

In small groups, affirm everyone by naming at least one ability they possess that makes them qualified to "apply" for the job of disciple.

Activity Ideas

The following activity ideas also relate to the Scripture readings. You may want to read the passage(s) indicated as part of the activity.

- Find a recipe for making homemade fortune cookies. After reading today's passage from Wisdom, invite the teens to scour the Scriptures for short, pithy examples of wisdom. They don't need to be limited to the Book of Wisdom. The Book of Proverbs is another great source. Instruct them to write or type these bits of wisdom on small slips of paper. Have fun together making fortune cookies and stuffing them with these scriptural fortunes. (Wis. 7:7–11)

- In the spirit of the passage from Hebrews, give each small group one of today's three readings or the psalm. After they read the passage together, direct them to answer the following questions:
  ○ What does this reading reveal about God?
  ○ What does this reading reveal about you?

  (Heb. 4:12–13)

- Invite the teens to pray Psalm 90 each day this week. Ask them to write a response to this question in their journal: What joys did Jesus bring you today? (Ps. 90:12–13,14–15,16–17)

- Challenge the teens to a proverb-writing contest. Encourage them to see which group can write the best modern version of Jesus' statement: "'It is easier for a camel to pass through a needle's eye than for a rich man to enter the kingdom of God.'" (Mark 10:17–30)

Twenty-ninth Sunday of the Year

Scripture Readings (147)
- ❖ Isa. 53:10–11
- ❖ Ps. 33:4–5,18–19,20,22
- ❖ Heb. 4:14–16
- ❖ Mark 10:35–45

God's Word

A major theme of the Scripture readings is "The suffering servant."

The first reading portrays a suffering servant following the will of God and being rewarded with exultation after being humiliated. Suffering can be a redeeming force. This reading foreshadows Jesus as a Suffering Servant who will give his life to save all of us. The reading also shows that our suffering does not go unnoticed or unrewarded by God.

The psalm is one to be prayed during times of suffering. It promises us salvation if we trust and hope in God's mercy and deliverance in the face of suffering and death.

The reading from the Letter to the Hebrews tells us that Jesus understands any suffering we may be going through because he has been through it himself. Even though Jesus is the great high priest, he has not put himself above us and the suffering we might experience. He is not distant from us.

The Gospel reading shows Jesus being faced with the ambition of James and John, who want to make sure they get positions of power in the Kingdom of God. Instead of getting angry at them, Jesus gives them a lesson in being disciples. Jesus teaches them that greatness comes from serving others, even to the point of suffering. Promotions or titles are absent in the Kingdom of God. Rank does not mean getting served; it means putting the needs of others first. Jesus promises first prize for taking last place.

Themes for Teens

The following themes from the Scriptures relate to the lives of teens:
- To lead, you must serve.
- To lead, you must suffer.
- The Lord is our protector.
- Jesus knows how we feel.
- Jesus awards first prize for being last.

Our Response

Activity

Winning the Real Prize

This activity is keyed to the Gospel reading. Set up a competition between teams of young people. Promise prizes and really encourage as much competition as you can. You can use relay races or games such as volleyball or basketball. Try to pick games that include everyone, but if that is not possible, assign the rest to be cheerleaders for specific teams.

After it is clear which team is the winner and which team is the loser, award the prize or prizes to the losers.

Read the Gospel reading for today together. Encourage the teens to discuss why Jesus awards first prize to those who finish last. How is that a radical change from the way we live in our society? Why is it okay not to have to win all the time?

Activity Ideas   The following activity ideas also relate to the Scripture readings. You may want to read the passage(s) indicated as part of the activity.

- Give each teen a copy of the popular poem "Footprints." Direct the teens to read the poem and respond in their journal in either of the following ways:
  ○ Talk to Jesus about something you are suffering through right now. Ask Jesus to walk with you through this tough time.
  ○ Talk to Jesus about someone you know who is suffering through a really tough time right now. Ask Jesus to walk with this person through this tough time.

(All readings)

- Provide the teens with craft materials to make a coupon book containing coupons for services—words, actions, or prayers—they will provide to their family this week. Have them make specific coupons for each family member to redeem. (Mark 10:35–45)

- Invite an adult or an older teen to talk to the group about her or his experience with suffering. Ask the volunteer to share answers to these questions:
  ○ How did you cope with the suffering?
  ○ How did God help you through this time?
  ○ Were there any blessings that came out of your suffering?

(All readings)

- Hang two pieces of poster board on the wall. Put a sign above one that says "First Place" and a sign above the other that says "Last Place." Give the teens some magazines and ask them to cut out pictures of people who are at the top in our society and glue these on the poster under the "First Place" sign. Also ask them to cut out pictures of people who are at the bottom in our society and glue these under the "Last Place" sign. Invite a teen to read aloud today's Gospel reading. Reverse the signs over the posters and ask the teens what they learned from the project and the reading. (Mark 10:35–45)

Thirtieth Sunday of the Year

Scripture Readings (150)

❖ Jer. 31:7–9
❖ Ps. 126:1–2,2–3,4–5,6
❖ Heb. 5:1–6
❖ Mark 10:46–52

God's Word

A major theme of the Scripture readings is "No one is turned away."

Jeremiah offers hope for persons who have been exiled from their home. The theme of deliverance shows special favor for anyone who is physically disabled or vulnerable in some way. This reading prophesies the time when Jesus will come and reach out to the outcasts of society and bring them home.

The psalm recounts the joy of the exiles when they finally return to their homeland. They pray for a deluge of blessings to replace their past suffering, and God comes through for them. Sorrow and weeping are tough to endure, but this psalm is hopeful that these will eventually be replaced by laughter and rejoicing.

The second reading sounds like a list of qualifications for Jesus' role as a high priest. His primary qualification is that of being human like us and having suffered the experience of being rejected and put to death.

In the Gospel reading, Jesus encounters the blind beggar Bartimaeus. Beggars were considered throwaways, but Jesus makes time for this one. Bartimaeus trusts Jesus as the Messiah and hopes in his mercy; Jesus says that Bartimaeus's faith made him well.

Themes for Teens

The following themes from the Scriptures relate to the lives of teens:
- We can come back home.
- Jesus welcomes outcasts.
- Jesus is on our side.
- Go to Jesus when you need help.
- Jesus helps us see.

Our Response

Activity

Learning to See Again

This activity is keyed to the Gospel reading. After sharing the Gospel, distribute a copy of the following poem to all the teens. After they read the poem, direct them to write their own prayer or poem inspired by the reading.

You may want to collect the prayers in a reflection booklet the teens could keep.

Dear God,
Please guide me always
in the path of your love.
To walk in the light
and shrug from the darkness.

Ordinary Time

Help me to never be blind
to real beauty:
the beauty in every raindrop,
in every soul, in every person.

Teach me
to look past the shiny wrappers
and discover
the treasure inside all of us.

Thank you, God,
for sharing your breath of life with me.
Strengthen me
to share this breath with others.
Amen.

(MaryAnn Taurino, Stella Maris High School,
Rockaway Park, NY, in Koch, ed., *More Dreams Alive,* p. 76)

Activity Ideas

The following activity ideas also relate to the Scripture readings. You may want to read the passage(s) indicated as part of the activity.

- Gather everyone in a circle for prayer and darken your gathering space. Give each person a taper candle and light one large candle in the center of the circle. After reading the Gospel, light the candle of someone in the circle and ask that person to say the prayer, "Lord help me to see." Continue this movement around the circle until all candles are lit and all have said the prayer. (Mark 10:46–52)

- Plan a visit to a nursing home, homeless shelter, or soup kitchen. After returning from the visit, ask the teens to compare their first impressions of the people they met with their impressions after they talked with them for a while. (Jer. 31:7–9; Mark 10:46–52)

- Encourage the teens to think of some of the people in their family, school, parish community, and world community who are in distress and need prayers. Invite the teens to write prayers of petition for these people. Pray the students' prayers during the next school or parish liturgy. (All readings)

- Give each teen a Bible with today's Gospel reading marked. Allow the teens plenty of space and quiet time to read the passage and reflect on the question, If Jesus asked you "What do you want me to do for you?" what would you say? (Mark 10:46–52)

Thirty-first Sunday of the Year

Scripture Readings (153)

- ❖ Deut. 6:2–6
- ❖ Ps. 18:2–3,3–4,47,51
- ❖ Heb. 7:23–28
- ❖ Mark 12:28–34

God's Word

A major theme of the Scripture readings is "Love God and your neighbor."

These readings challenge us to put our love for God first, then to spread that love to our neighbors.

In Deuteronomy, Moses tells the people that fear of the Lord and love of the Lord are a recipe for a long, prosperous life. Moses makes it clear that just following the Law is not enough. The Law is to be followed as an expression of love for God and neighbor. It takes one's entire being—heart, soul, and strength—to truly love God.

The psalmist sees loving God as the source of strength and safety. God is strong and unmovable, a rock to hide behind, where we will be safe from our enemies, in whatever form they threaten us.

The reading from the Letter to the Hebrews continues the theme of God's love revealed and given in Jesus, who goes to the Father on our behalf like a great high priest. The writer of Hebrews takes great pains to explain that Jesus is not like the other high priests. His sacrifice is once and for all. He is holy, innocent, undefiled, and higher than the heavens.

The reading from Mark opens with the Pharisees using questions to set a trap for Jesus. They ask Jesus which commandment is the most important. Jesus responds by quoting Deuteronomy, which says that God is God alone and we are to love God with our entire being. Then Jesus adds a second important commandment: "'You shall love your neighbor as yourself.'" Jesus' view of the Commandments is that they are specifications of the great commandment to love God and our neighbor—that if we obey the Commandments we are, in fact, loving God and our neighbor.

The Pharisee recognizes that love of God, self, and neighbor are more important to God than empty rituals and blind obedience to laws.

Themes for Teens

The following themes from the Scriptures relate to the lives of teens:

- Love the Lord with your entire self.
- Love your neighbor.
- Love yourself.
- The Lord is my rock.

Our Response

Activity   **R-e-s-p-e-c-t**

This poster activity is keyed to the Gospel reading. It shows in a concrete way how we need to revere God, ourselves, and others.

Give each teen a stick-on name tag and a fine-tipped marker. Ask them to write the letters *R, E, S, P, E, C,* and *T* vertically on the tag. Introduce the activity in the following way:

> In today's readings, we are told to love our neighbor as ourselves. How do you show respect for yourself? Do you treat yourself like the gift from God you truly are? Use the letters on your tag as an acrostic. For each letter, write one word or phrase that describes ways you can show respect for yourself.

Direct the teens to do this individually and to wear the tag for the rest of the session.

Next, form the teens into groups of six and give them a large piece of newsprint or white construction paper and several markers. Direct them to write the letters *R, E, S, P, E, C,* and *T* vertically down the center of the paper. Continue with the following instructions:

> Now that we have some insight on how to love ourselves, let's move on to the way we should treat our neighbors. Do you treat your friends and family and the other people around you with respect? Do you treat them like the gifts from God they truly are? Use the letters on your poster as an acrostic. For each letter, write one word or phrase that describes ways you can show respect for others.

Direct the teens to include everyone in their group in this discussion.

Last, gather the teens in one large group. Cover one wall of your meeting space with a large piece of butcher paper. Make markers available. Write the letters *R, E, S, P, E, C,* and *T* in huge letters, covering the length of the wall. Continue:

> We have reflected on how we must love ourselves and discussed how we should love others. Now let's turn our attention to the way we should treat God. Do you treat God with respect? Are you grateful for all the wonderful gifts God has given you? Think of words and phrases beginning with the letters *R, E, S, P, E, C,* or *T* that describe ways we can show respect for God.

As the teens think of ideas and share them with the group, invite them to write the ideas on the paper near the letter that corresponds with the first letter of their word(s).

Close by asking the teens to use these ideas as concrete ways to live out the great commandments given to us by Jesus in the Gospel.

Activity Ideas   The following activity ideas also relate to the Scripture readings. You may want to read the passage(s) indicated as part of the activity.

- After reading about the importance of loving our neighbor as ourselves, divide the teens into pairs for an affirmation activity. First, ask the teens to share with their partner one good quality about themselves. Next, direct them to identify at least one good quality about their partner. Ask each pair to join with another pair and repeat the affirmations. (Mark 12:28–34)

- In their journal, have the teens write about some of the ways they love God . . .
  - with their whole heart
  - with their whole soul
  - with their whole mind
  - with all their strength

(Deut. 6:2–6; Mark 12:28–34)

- God is referred to in today's psalm as the rock we can rely on. Encourage the teens to find rock music songs that have messages we can relate to the image of Jesus as a rock of strength. You may also want to ask them to play snippets of songs that relate to the theme of loving our neighbors. (Ps. 18:2–3,3–4,47,51)

- The reading from Hebrews stresses the importance of approaching God, the Father, through Jesus. Jesus taught his disciples to approach God as a father. Ask the teens to pray together the Lord's Prayer, stopping after each line for a few moments of quiet reflection on what the words of this popular prayer really mean. (Heb. 7:23–28)

Thirty-second Sunday of the Year

Scripture Readings (156)

- ❖ 1 Kings 17:10–16
- ❖ Ps. 146:7,8–9,9–10
- ❖ Heb. 9:24–28
- ❖ Mark 12:38–44

God's Word

A major theme of the Scriptures readings is "Giving what we have."

In the First Book of Kings, we read of a widow who has so little that she fears she and her son will soon die. Elijah, the prophet, sets aside her fears and asks her to prepare some food for him and for herself and her son. Elijah then tells her that God will not allow her flour jar to go empty or her oil jug to run dry. God indeed smiles on her generosity to a stranger, and it is as Elijah said—they all have enough to eat for a year.

The psalmist praises the Lord as the God who provides food and drink for the hungry and thirsty but also liberty for prisoners, sight for the blind, and safety for the widow and orphan.

The reading from the Letter to the Hebrews points out that Christ's one sacrifice is sufficient for the atonement of everyone because it is the perfect and complete giving of self for others.

In the Gospel reading, Jesus expresses disdain for people with abundance who go to the Temple and give to charity only for public show. Jesus is touched by a widow who has little to give, but gives of the little she has. Jesus is so impressed that he calls over the disciples to watch and learn from her.

Both widows—the one in the first reading and the one in the Gospel—give of what little they have—a true giving of one's self. That kind of generosity is life-giving and is great in God's eyes.

Ordinary Time

Themes for Teens The following themes from the Scriptures relate to the lives of teens:
- Be welcoming to strangers.
- Jesus will come again.
- God speaks through prophets.
- God keeps promises.
- Giving of what you have promises rewards of lasting value.

Our Response

Activity **Where Does Your Money Go?**

This activity is keyed to the Gospel reading. It asks the young people to consider changing how they spend their money, in order to follow the example of the generous widow in the Gospel.

In advance, direct everyone to bring change for a dollar with them to the meeting. Tell them to make sure they have quarters, dimes, nickels, and pennies that all add up to a dollar. Make sure you have additional change available for teens who forget to bring change or need to make further change from the coins they bring.

Have the teens make a list of all the things they spend their money on. Then ask them to take a look at their list of expenses and to divide their dollar up based on how much of each dollar goes to each type of item on the list. For example, twenty-five cents goes for food, ten cents for movies, fifty cents for clothes, and so forth.

After the teens have divided up their change, have them share their results in small groups.

To conclude, read the Gospel passage and ask what Jesus was trying to teach by holding up the widow as an example. Direct the teens to turn their attention back to their money and consider any alterations they might make in the way they spend it. Question whether they are giving anything to the poor or homeless, or to support their parish community.

Activity Ideas The following activity ideas also relate to the Scripture readings. You may want to read the passage(s) indicated as part of the activity.

- After the teens have reflected on the first reading, direct them to write a response in their journal to this question: How would you react if someone offered you a year's supply of groceries if you would simply share a sandwich with them? (1 Kings 17:10–16)

- Introduce the teens to the concept of stewardship in terms of sharing time, talent, and treasure with others in the parish community. Challenge them to compare what they receive from their parish community and what they give back. Invite them to make at least a small commitment of time (perhaps to help with a parish ministry), talent (to offer a gift—such as music or drawing), or treasure (to give an amount of money each week for parish support). (1 Kings 17:10–16; Ps. 146:7,8–9,9–10; Mark 12:38–44)

- Encourage the teens to think about the financial difficulty of elderly citizens living on fixed incomes. Ask your pastor or parish staff member for the names of some elderly parishioners who could use a helping hand. Divide the young people into teams to do yard work, housecleaning, or meal preparation for some of these folks, who will probably enjoy the company as well as the help. (1 Kings 17:10–16; Mark 12:38–44)

Thirty-third Sunday of the Year

Scripture Readings (159)

❖ Dan. 12:1–3
❖ Ps. 16:5,8,9–10,11
❖ Heb. 10:11–14,18
❖ Mark 13:24–32

God's Word

A major theme of the Scripture readings is "Be prepared for the day of the Lord."

Daniel, seeking a way to keep fellow Jews loyal, writes about the harsh reality of God's Second Coming and how only the just will survive. At the same time, he offers the hope of reward, even beyond death, for those who are faithful. This is one of the earliest references to resurrection after death.

The psalm is a plea, on the part of the just, for safety and protection in the time of the Lord's coming. The psalmist, rather than walking in the ways of his own choosing, asks God to point out the path of life to walk.

The writer of the Letter to the Hebrews assures the listeners that they have been saved by the one sacrifice of Jesus, that repetition of former kinds of sacrifice are not necessary, and that trust in Jesus is the assurance of their salvation.

The Gospel also refers to the end time. Jesus' words and descriptions must have really shaken the disciples when they heard them. Jesus was talking about the end of this world as well as the events surrounding his death. Only God knows when the world will end, and God will save those who are faithful to the end.

Although these descriptions of the end are scary, they also come with promises. Because of Jesus we need not fear our death or the end of the world. He has promised us life everlasting. We are not to be filled with constant anxiety. Rather, we are to be prepared and alert for God's coming, whenever and however it takes place.

Themes for Teens

The following themes from the Scriptures relate to the lives of teens:
- God keeps us safe.
- Show us the path of life.
- Jesus is our sacrifice.
- No one knows the hour God will come.
- Be prepared for God's coming.

Our Response

Activity

Will You Be Ready?

This journal reflection activity is keyed to the Gospel reading. It asks the teens to look at their readiness to meet Jesus in light of their own mortality. Writing your own obituary can be an eye-opening experience.

Give the teens each a copy of today's Gospel reading. Give them plenty of space to spread out and plenty of quiet time to read the passage and reflect on it.

Direct them to write their own obituary—what they hope it will say about them at the end of their life. It should reflect the kind of life they are planning to live.

Conclude by offering them this challenge: As the Gospel says, we do not know the day or the hour that God will come for us. Will we be ready?

Activity Ideas

The following activity ideas also relate to the Scripture readings. You may want to read the passage(s) indicated as part of the activity.

- Sing the song "Path of Life," by Mike Balhoff, Gary Daigle, and Darryl Ducote (*Glory and Praise,* vol. 3, no. 226). Talk about young people's struggle to discover their vocation in life. Affirm that it is okay to be searching for what they want to be when they become an adult, even though it is frustrating sometimes. Urge them to rely on God to help them discern their path through life. (Ps. 16:5,8,9–10,11)

- Ask a peer counselor or a staff member of a Catholic social agency in your area to come speak to your group. Start a discussion about the events that make it seem like the world is crashing down on us—the suicide of a friend, the breakup of a relationship, drug abuse, teen pregnancy, the divorce of a parent, and the like. Stress with the teens the importance of talking to others when they get overanxious and discouraged. Give them plenty of contacts and strategies they can use to help themselves or a friend in trouble. (Dan. 12:1–3; Ps. 16:5,8,9–10,11; Mark 13:24–32)

- Direct the teens to close their eyes and quietly reflect on a time and place in their life when they really felt God's presence. As they quietly meditate, ask them to return to that place and time in their thoughts and recall what God was trying to share with them. Encourage the use of meditative prayer to get in better touch with God. (Ps. 16:5,8,9–10,11)

- Share a prayer of petition with your group. Pray the psalm together and then offer the names of people in your life who need God to help keep them safe. Ask the rest of the group to hold these people in their prayers for the rest of the week. (Ps. 16:5,8,9–10,11)

Thirty-fourth Sunday of the Year (Christ the King)

Scripture Readings (162)

❖ Dan. 7:13–14
❖ Ps. 93:1,1–2,5
❖ Rev. 1:5–8
❖ John 18:33–37

God's Word

A major theme of the Scriptures readings is "Christ the King."

The first reading from Daniel foreshadows the return of the Risen Christ as a king sent by God to rule the people. Unlike earthly royalty, who lose their thrones to warring foes or death, Christ's kingship is everlasting. God's Kingdom is described here and in the responsorial psalm as encompassing all on earth and in heaven.

The psalmist sees the Lord in the attire and tribute fitting for a king. However, this king does not wears robes of fine material, but is clothed in strength, trust, and holiness.

The Book of Revelation reveals to us more about the relationship between Jesus and his Father. Jesus is called first a faithful witness—one who witnesses his Father to the world and remains faithful to him. As king over all, Jesus frees captives to serve God as Father. Jesus came first to serve others. But his Second Coming will be in majesty, as on a cloud. Although many kings lose their throne to death, Jesus began his rule through a death that led to our salvation.

In the Gospel reading, Jesus is interrogated by Pilate. Jesus tells him that he is indeed a king but not like the kings and kingdoms of this world. He is not the type of king the people expected or the type authorities of that day would accept. Jesus comes to testify to the truth, meaning that he belongs to God and God's Kingdom, and that all who believe in him also belong to God and God's Kingdom.

We accept Jesus as King and enter the Kingdom of God when we hear and follow the truth of his Word.

Themes for Teens

The following themes from the Scriptures relate to the lives of teens:
- Christ is our King.
- Jesus' Reign never ends.
- God is the beginning and the end.
- Jesus is the truth.
- The Kingdom is coming.

Our Response

Activity

To Tell You the Truth

This activity is keyed to the Gospel reading. Note that Jesus says he has come to testify to the truth. Explain that the truth Jesus was referring to was not so much in terms of being honest and telling the truth as it was in recognizing and living according to the foundational truths about God and about being human. Examples of these truths are that God created us all in God's image and likeness, that we are worthy of respect and reverence, that we are responsible for one another as brothers and sisters in the Lord, that to gain life we have to give it in service, and that sin in the world is overcome by service.

Then ask the teens to think of some situations in their own life—in school, at work, with family, with friends—where it might be tough to live these truths. Divide the teens into small groups and direct them to prepare to act out a situation in which they might feel challenged to live the truths Jesus referred to.

After the small groups have presented their skits, call for suggestions on how to deal with each situation in a truthful way. Here are some possible situations: minority students being excluded from groups, a student from a poor family not having suitable clothing, a couple of students who are constantly disrupting class, and persons who are constantly cursing and using foul language directed at others.

Activity Ideas   The following activity ideas also relate to the Scripture readings. You may want to read the passage(s) indicated as part of the activity.

- How does God rule? Contrast one day in the life of a modern-day king or the President of the United States with one day in the life of Jesus Christ. How does Jesus defy all the stereotypes of a ruler? (All readings)

- King is only one of the many titles given to Jesus in the Scriptures. Divide the teens into groups and challenge them to find other names for Jesus. Have them make a list of the names and their respective Scripture citations. Share all the lists with the entire group. You may want to combine the lists and make copies for the entire group to use for future Scripture study. (All readings)

- Instead of reading a psalm that praises Jesus as King, make a praise banner to hang in your meeting space. Cut out felt letters to spell "Praise Jesus, Our King." Cut out colorful symbols from felt to represent all the wonderful gifts God has given to us. Glue them on the banner surrounding the words. (Ps. 93:1,1–2,5)

- How do we honor a king? How do we honor Jesus? Talk about the ways our society honors presidents, kings, or dignitaries. Contrast this with the type of honor our King Jesus would want. Direct everyone to think of a way they could honor Jesus with their words and actions. Then ask the teens to think of a way, as a group, they can honor Jesus with their words and actions. (All readings)

Audiovisual Distributors

Bridgestone Multimedia
300 North McKemy Avenue
Chandler, AZ 85226
800-523-0988
fax 602-438-2702

Liguori Publications
1 Liguori Drive
Liguori, MO 63057-9999
800-325-9521

Mars Hill Productions
9302 Wilcrest
Houston, TX 77099
800-231-0629

Resources

Catucci, Thomas F. *Time with Jesus: Twenty Guided Meditations for Youth.*
    Notre Dame, IN: Ave Maria Press, 1993.
Faley, Roland J. *Footprints on the Mountain: Preaching and Teaching the
    Sunday Readings.* Mahwah, NJ: Paulist Press, 1994.
Hamma, Robert M. "The Lectionary: Heart of the Bible." *Catholic Update*
    (St. Anthony Messenger Press, Cincinnati, OH), C1090, 1990.
———, ed. *A Catechmen's Lectionary.* Mahwah, NJ: Paulist Press, 1988.
Harris, Maria. *Fashion Me a People: Curriculum in the Church.* Louisville, KY:
    Westminster/John Knox Press, 1989.
Homily Service: An Ecumenical Resource for Sharing the Word. Cycle B, vol.
    26, nos. 9–12, and vol. 27, no. 1-8, 1993–94. Available from the Liturgical
    Conference, 8750 Georgia Avenue, Suite 123, Silver Spring, MD 20910-
    3621.
National Federation for Catholic Youth Ministry (NFCYM). *The Challenge of
    Adolescent Catechesis: Maturing in Faith.* Washington, DC: NFCYM, 1986.
———. *The Challenge of Catholic Youth Evangelization: Called to Be
    Witnesses and Storytellers.* New Rochelle, NY: Don Bosco Multimedia, 1993.
Pontifical Bible Commission. "The Interpretation of the Bible in the Church."
    Origins 23, no. 29, 6 January 1994.
Sanchez, Patricia Datchuck. *The Word We Celebrate: Commentary on the
    Sunday Lectionary, Years A, B, and C.* Kansas City, MO: Sheed and Ward,
    1989.
Smith, Virginia. "If I Can Find My Bible, What Do I Do Next?" *Youth Update*
    (St. Anthony Messenger Press), December 1990.
United States Catholic Conference (USCC). *The Bible in Catechesis, The
    Living Light.* Washington, DC: Department of Education, USCC, n.d.

Index of Themes

Index of Gospel Readings

Acknowledgments (*continued*)

The scriptural quotations marked NRSV are from the New Revised Standard Version of the Bible, copyright © 1989 by the Division of Christian Education of the National Council of the Churches of Christ in the United States of America. All rights reserved.

All other scriptural quotations are from the New American Bible. Copyright © 1970 by the Confraternity of Christian Doctrine, 3211 Fourth Street NE, Washington, DC 20017. All rights reserved.

The excerpt on page 7 is from *The Challenge of Catholic Youth Evangelization: Called to Be Witnesses and Storytellers,* by the National Federation for Catholic Youth Ministry (NFCYM) (New Rochelle, NY: Don Bosco Multimedia, 1993), pages 5–6. Copyright © 1993 by the NFCYM.

The keys to Scripture study on page 11 are from *Fashion Me a People: Curriculum in the Church,* by Maria Harris (Louisville, KY: Westminster/John Knox Press, 1989), pages 60–61. Copyright © 1989 by Westminster/John Knox Press.

The excerpt by Pope Paul VI on page 18 is quoted from *A Catechumen's Lectionary,* edited by Robert M. Hamma (Mahwah, NJ: Paulist Press, 1988), page 19. Copyright © 1988 by the Missionary Society of Saint Paul the Apostle in the State of New York.

The prayer from the Divine Office on page 19 is adapted from *Christian Prayer: The Liturgy of the Hours,* translated by the International Commission on English in the Liturgy (ICEL) (New York: Catholic Book Publishing Co., 1976), page 696. Copyright © 1976 by the ICEL.

The profession of faith on page 31 is from the English translation of the *Rite of Christian Initiation of Adults,* in *The Rites of the Catholic Church,* volume 1, study edition, translated by the ICEL (New York: Pueblo Publishing Company, 1990), pages 401–402. Copyright © 1985 by the ICEL. Used with permission. All rights reserved.

The information about cyber confession on page 41 is from "Cyber Confession: Digital Priest Ready to Absolve Sins," by Katharine McKee, *Newport News Daily Press,* 27 September 1995, page C2.

The excerpt by Cecil B. De Mille on page 50 is quoted from *More Sower's Seeds: Second Planting,* by Brian Cavanaugh, TOR (Mahwah, NJ: Paulist Press, 1992), pages 41–42. Copyright © 1992 by Brian Cavanaugh. Used with permission of Brian Cavanaugh.

The poem "Touch" on page 90 is from *The Calm Beneath the Storm,* by Donal Neary, SJ (Chicago: Loyola University Press, 1984), pages 10–11. Copyright © 1983 by Donal Neary, SJ. Used with permission.

The prayer on pages 123–124 is from *More Dreams Alive: Prayers by Teenagers,* edited by Carl Koch (Winona, MN: Saint Mary's Press, 1995), page 76. Copyright © 1995 by Saint Mary's Press. All rights reserved.